Awaken

Awaken Your All Knowing Heart

Rosalie Deer Heart

BALBOA
PRESS

A DIVISION OF HAY HOUSE

Balboa Press books may be ordered through booksellers or by contacting:

Balboa Press
A Division of Hay House
1663 Liberty Drive
Bloomington, IN 47403
www.balboapress.com
1-(877) 407-4847

Because of the dynamic nature of the Internet, any web addresses or links contained in this book may have changed since publication and may no longer be valid. The views expressed in this work are solely those of the author and do not necessarily reflect the views of the publisher, and the publisher hereby disclaims any responsibility for them.

The author of this book does not dispense medical advice or prescribe the use of any technique as a form of treatment for physical, emotional, or medical problems without the advice of a physician, either directly or indirectly. The intent of the author is only to offer information of a general nature to help you in your quest for emotional and spiritual well-being. In the event you use any of the information in this book for yourself, which is your constitutional right, the author and the publisher assume no responsibility for your actions.

Any people depicted in stock imagery provided by Thinkstock are models, and such images are being used for illustrative purposes only.
Certain stock imagery © Thinkstock.

ISBN: 978-1-4525-3737-5 (e)
ISBN: 978-1-4525-3629-3 (sc)
ISBN: 978-1-4525-3628-6 (hc)

Library of Congress Control Number: 2011911887

Printed in the United States of America

Balboa Press rev. date: 7/18/2011

Dedication

To Malia and Noah,

My beloved grandchildren, who were born knowing how to live in the present as well as modeling how to bridge into the future with grace and humor.

Contents

Acknowledgments

To Nancy Carlson for her love, support, and meticulous pursuit of misspelled words, extra spaces, and superfluous commas.

To Alison Strickland for her love and focus on the multitude of organizational details and insistence that I trust my own voice.

To Ed and Leslie Rosenberg for their love, their three day focused retreat, and their continual reminders that love was my message.

To Daniel Holeman for his visionary art and his delightful presence on this planet.

To the library angels at the Scarborough, Maine Library: Deirdre Larson, Kate Callahan, Marilyn Taylor, Catherine Morrison, and Laurel Cox, for their hospitality and book referrals.

To Debbie Lozito of the Edythe Dyer Library in Hampden, Maine, for her hospitality and for referring to me as "our writer in residence."

To the student writers in Mrs. LaPointe's first grade class at Hermon Elementary School in Hermon, Maine, for reminding me how much I love to teach, write, and laugh: Luke Sherman, Janie Snow, Aidan Tremblay, Corbin Wescott, Malakye Ouellette, Cady Parent, Noah Martinez, Madison Higgins, Parker Edwards, Melaina Eaton, Kaden Downs, Nevaeh Davis, Sydney Gallop, Jack Mailloux, Marin McPhee, and James Desjardins.

To my spiritual guides and teachers who insisted that I write this book and nurtured me with guidance throughout the journey.

Preface

This book is both a statement and a reflection about my own spiritual journey. As I write in the introduction, journaling has been my familiar practice for almost forty years. When I write, my words become like mirrors that I can look into and reflect on what is happening within myself.

After much encouragement from my friends, I agreed to include personal stories from my journals in this book. Each story is true. Some of them may seem "far out" or even unbelievable. I did not invite the specific experiences that I recorded as stories in my journal. However, in retrospect, I acknowledged saying "yes" to opening my heart and surrendering to the mysteries. Allowing myself to be open to the unknown was new for me and I was frightened at times. However, I intuitively recognized the rightness of stepping into the unknown. Eventually, I grew the habit of leading my life with full courage until boldness developed into a value. My consciousness expanded and I embraced a different reality. Alice Walker, author of *The Color Purple,* echoes my experience when she writes, "I can only persist in being myself."

As you read my stories, I invite you to respond with your all-knowing heart. I hope my stories ignite a spark within you to recollect and remember intuitive experiences that you have forgotten or denied. Write down your own connections or unanswered questions. If you are feeling creative and daring, make up your own multidimensional stories and commit to live into your story's theme. Eventually, you too will be a magnet for "far out" experiences that will challenge what you believe is possible. Please be patient with yourself if you have not yet said "yes" to the unfolding of your multidimensional nature. Some people welcome spiritual guides, angels, fairies, inner earth beings, and even extra-terrestrials as aspects of their multidimensional reality.

A long time ago, someone suggested that one of the reasons we do not expect miracles is because we do not live in a miracle consciousness culture. I believe that we can each grow into our multidimensional consciousness by paying attention to and honoring our blink truths—intuitive flashes, serendipities, and vivid dreams—and by sharing our personal stories. We grow collective consciousness when we share our personal consciousnesses. Each story adds to a continuum of possibilities until we take our multidimensional natures for granted.

Mary Oliver, one of my favorite poets, writes, "A book is a path of words, which takes the heart in a new direction." Each chapter in this book invites you to open your heart and take up residency in your high heart, which is an energy center midway between your human heart and your throat. I do my best to encourage you to surrender your small, adapted version of yourself and embrace your expanded, authentic self. Since we cannot sit down together and share our journeys, I offer this book as an interactive guidebook. If we were sitting together watching the sun rise or set, I might tell you a story, and then you might share one of your own. The conversation would deepen, and we would each feel fuller and more connected to one another as well as to our unique journeys. With each story and reflection, we would add our personal energies to the expansion of collective consciousness.

I sprinkled questions and activities throughout each chapter for you to interact with because that's how you can record and deepen your own voice and vision. To invite ideas, connections, insights, and revelations, you will find reflective questions and journal prompts at the end of each chapter. When an idea or a question taps at your all-knowing heart, please write as if you are dying. People who are dying usually speak their deepest truths because they have nothing to lose. Be honest. Challenge yourself to access your inner wisdom. Here are some general journaling guidelines to consider as you begin taking your own journey to heart:

- Breathe into your high heart, the energy center that is midway between your human heart and your throat, before writing. As you inhale, say "yes," and as you exhale say "thank you."
- Write without thinking about correct spelling or punctuation. Remember you can return to your words to add more details and correct errors.

- Write from the edges of what you know. Give yourself the gift of writing what you do <u>not</u> know yet as well as what you are coming to know.
- Be open to your future by sprinkling "why not?" and "what if?" into your journals.
- Enjoy the process of connecting with your soul.

Introduction

Today at the library I bumped into a woman whose son went to high school with my daughter twenty years ago. She asked me what I was doing with my life now. I summarized the book I was writing. She smiled and said, "Rosalie, you are creating a collage of your adult life." She is an artist and thinks in terms of collages and montages and weavings. However, the more I mulled over her insightful observation, the more aligned I felt with the truth behind her words. In my thirties, women's adult psychology and creativity were my passions. In my fourth decade, spiritual psychology and community reigned. The decade of my fifties brought a passion for quantum physics, evolution, mysticism, and sculpting. Healing became the focus in my sixties. Intuition and journaling were always the main threads in the weaving of my life. Thank you, Karen Perry, for naming the obvious for me. And now for the claiming!

Ronette Every Stoddard, a gifted psychic and friend, told me nearly half my life ago that my destiny required me to write inspirational books that opened people up to the many dimensions that exist outside of space and time. For years I convinced myself that she had made a mistake. I reach out to her now in spirit to say "Thank you for the push, Sweetie." Although each book I have written contained some inspiration, I know this is the one! Plus, I already have the title for my next inspirational book: *The Future Is a Frequency.* Although my name is the only one that appears on the cover, please appreciate that many of my words were informed, guided, and graced by guides who reside in many dimensions.

There is a profound difference between growing up and waking up. There is also a profound difference between naming and claiming. When you name something, you recognize what is already there. When you claim it, you dare to act on your knowing and your values become integrated with your voice and your vision. This book is about the expansion of consciousness through love. Love is an action verb. Love grounds and uplifts. Love extends across dimensions. Love insists on embracing its own reflection. Love links us to our futures.

Listen in on the wisdom perspective of my guides:

You are living within the parenthesis, the in-between place between the past and the future. It is a place rich in possibilities, fantasies, projections, hopes and fears.

It carries the potential to be a sacred place of healing or a place of attachment and suffering.

If you align with your soul, the future will enfold you with blessings, beauty, and multidimensional surprises.

If you align with your ego, the future will be crowded with disappointments, struggles, and karmic pain. The choice is yours.

Love lurks everywhere. Love is a rainbow bridge that connects us to God. Love melts all that does not resonate with its frequency. Love is for giving and love is forgiving. Love is an ever-expanding spiral. Love asks for everything. Yet without love's presence, we are nothing. So love's only question is: how much love and light do you dare to embody?

I invite you to wrap your knowing heart around the following questions:

- What would happen if you surrounded yourself with forgiveness for any mistakes you have made from the beginning of time?
- What would happen if you banished fear from your consciousness?
- What would happen if you released karmic past lifetime overlays and let go of all stored up emotions in order to live your present life more fully?
- What would happen if you accessed your unique energetic soul blueprint to assist you in fulfilling your emergent evolutionary soul purpose?
- What would happen if you remembered how to access your healing blueprints and accepted responsibility for your own wellbeing?

- What would happen if you chose, in this moment, to make the remainder of your life a prayer and dedicated your life to serving the emergent future?

I wrote this book to encourage you to reflect, explore, and claim all of who you are. Our spiritual journeys last a lifetime, so we all have plenty of time. I welcome you to your journey toward authentic self and send you love, gratitude and blessings for being present on this earth at this crucial time in our history. My prayer is this: May we all be instruments of love, understanding, and peace.

Section One

The Heart of Love

Chapter One

Love

"The human heart can go to the lengths of God."
- Christopher Fry

The Meanings of Love

Everyone thinks they understand the meaning of the simple four letter word "Love." Yet when I asked five people to define love, I was surprised to hear five different meanings. Mystics believe that love is the evolutionary engine of the universe, while scientists describe love as the connecting glue that unifies consciousness. Religious leaders embrace love as a synonym for God, while some researchers describe love as the heart's intelligence. Poets describe love as a transforming power, while philosophers refer to love as the essence of the soul. Being awake and being love are the two great themes in literature. In addition, love is the central belief in all of the world's religions. Love is the force behind the will of God. Has anyone told you that Love is also the most searched word on the Internet or that in Sanskrit, the basis for most East Indian languages, there are 96 words for love?

To me, loving is a state of being. It is a way of relating to people and the world in nurturing, supporting, and forgiving ways. Nourishment, which is another word for love, is essential to our wellbeing. As we explore the many facets of love together, I hope you can deepen your own understanding and appreciation of the presence of love in your life.

The School of Love

Let's wrap our arms and our hearts around the principle that we are students in the School of Love. Love is the teacher. Learning how to be present for love without controlling or being controlled is one of the essential courses. Growing in love and learning how to be awake and remain awake comprise the core curriculum. Awakening to your authentic, loving nature and being true to your soul's path and mission expands your consciousness.

Self-knowledge and self-love mark the beginning of your spiritual journey. Self-love empowers you to trust in your own direction and to take action. The first step in cultivating love as a spiritual practice is to remember that love is your nature and like all abilities we must use it to grow it. The only way to develop our love muscles is by loving.

The Lesson of Self-Love

The one you have the most influence with in the present as well as the future is yourself. Are you willing to extend love and compassion to yourself? Did you know that self-hatred is prevalent in the United States? Culturally we are trained to be critical of ourselves.

Please remember that the more you surround yourself with love, the more love you have to give others. Increasing your love for yourself before you extend love to another creates an irresistible frequency that deepens your experience of the present and beckons the future. Many of us have perfected over-loving and over-giving as a way of feeling loved. In order to awaken the all-knowing heart, we need to move from self-sacrifice to self-love. Then self-actualization becomes the next challenge.

Filling up and spilling over with love empowers. Instead of giving love when you are only half full or less, you gift others from your overflowing saucer, never from a half empty cup. The principle is overflow. You never give more love than you have. By keeping your heart open to love, and by being a channel for love, you will attract more love into your life. Experiment with loving yourself at each moment as already perfect. If you want more love in your life, become more loving. You influence what you attract in your future by your present beliefs.

George Leonard, author of *The Life We Are Given: A Long Term Program for Realizing the Potential of Body, Mind, and Soul,* invites us to "Love something and watch it blossom." I invite each of us to adopt ourselves as the person to love and to watch ourselves blossom!

❖ List all the various forms of love that exist in your life. After each item, identify the meaning that each aspect of love has in your life. Remember that love is not the goal; it is the cause of everything.

❖ What do I need to say, do, release, or remember in order to love myself more deeply?

❖ What can I do in this moment to practice self-loving?

Love's Choices

Loving is a transformational process. Love moves you beyond where you might be comfortable and asks that you become more of who you are becoming. For example, whenever I do a soul reading, I move into my heart, and the person with whom I am consulting becomes my beloved. When I connect with my beloved heart to heart, I become a channel for guidance.

The choices we make about love define our lives. Recently, I made a choice to welcome a sick cat into our home because I did not want her to die in a shelter. We have all treated Tinkerbelle to banquets of love and she has returned our love in kind.

Welcoming all that arises with love is another one of love's principles. If we look for the love strand in each of our encounters, we can usually find it. This takes practice because we are not brought up to be aware of the presence of love. However, when you remind yourself to see through the eyes of love, your perspective changes and expands.

When you embody the affirmation: "Love guides my life," then any part of your life that exists outside of love will confront you in order to remind you of your commitment. For example, I am fine affirming love until a driver cuts in front of me. Then my anger takes over. If I hold onto my anger, I will forget to reconnect with my loving intention. Be prepared to welcome love's polarities such as fear, anger, jealousy, cynicism, and apathy when you affirm love. I remind myself and others to laugh when love's opposite arises because we have an opportunity to integrate or transform an emotion by surrounding it with love. These emotions are teachers. When any of love's polarities arise, notice them without energizing them and return to love as your foundation. Love invites you to do your work and return to the wholeness of your heart. I invite you to open your heart to the wisdom of poet Rainer Maria Rilke. "To love is to cast light, to be loved means to be ablaze."

Listen in on this conversation about love between my two grandchildren:

"How are families made?" asked Noah, age 5.

"By love," his 9-year-old sister, Malia, replied before I thought of an answer. "And even if the mother and father grow out of love with each other, they each still love us and we are still a family even if we don't all live together anymore and even if they marry someone else and we get another adult to love us and be our family."

Later the same week Malia put love into action when Noah announced he had lost his first tooth. Malia remembered how special losing her first tooth was, and she secretly took a ten-dollar bill from her piggy bank and put it next to Noah's letter to the tooth fairy. The next morning I was perplexed when the extra ten dollars appeared. Malia took me aside and told me she wanted Noah to have a special memory of his first lost tooth. Love surprises.

Heart Dynamics

The heart begins to form in the fetus before the brain. Our human heart is the deepest place of listening and receiving information in our physical body. It is where we awaken to love and receive wisdom. Our heart is also central to our health and wellbeing. Did you know that your heart's magnetic field is more than 5,000 times stronger that that of your brain? Every beat of your heart carries intricate messages that affect your emotions, physical health, and the quality of your life experiences.

Our heart profoundly affects perception, awareness, and intelligence. Our heart also creates oxytocin, commonly referred to as the "love" or "bonding" hormone. Concentrations of oxytocin in the heart are as high as those found in the brain.

According to Doc Childre and Howard Martin, researchers at HeartMath, located in Boulder Creek, California, as we learn to become more heart-centered, we may be surprised by new and enhanced mental clarity, productivity, physical energy, positive attitudes, and satisfaction with the quality of our work.

Heart-Centered Consciousness

Consciousness is connected to the body through the heart chakra. The heart is the largest generator of electromagnetic energy in our body and produces, sends, and receives a broad spectrum of other types and frequencies of energies. Awakening through the heart connects one to the wisdom dimension, where all truth is known.

The heart and brain maintain a continuous two-way dialogue, each influencing the other's functioning. Although it is not well known, the heart sends far more information to the brain than the brain sends to the heart, and the signals the heart sends to the brain can influence perception, emotional processing, and higher cognitive functions. The heart also generates the strongest rhythmic electromagnetic field in the body and this can actually be measured in the brain waves of people around us. According to Paul Pearsall, author of *The Heart's Code*, "The heart has its own form of wisdom that is different from the rational brain, but every bit as important to living, loving, working, and healing."

Touch Dynamics

Touch is fundamental to human communications, bonding, and good health. As Americans, our culture suffers from touch deprivation. I remember being stunned when I read a multicultural research report on touching by Dr. Sidney Jourard, author of *The Transparent Self*. He studied the conversations of friends in different parts of the world as they sat in cafes together. In England, two friends did not touch at all during the hour. In the United States, friends reached out to touch each other two times in an hour. In France, friends touched 110 times in an hour. Puerto Rico took the prize for touching with an astounding 180 touches in one hour. Virginia Satir, mentor and author of *Peoplemaking*, emphasizes the power of touching when she writes, "We need four hugs a day for survival. We need eight hugs a day for maintenance. We need twelve hugs a day for growth."

- ❖ How is your hug quotient for this day?
- ❖ Challenge yourself to collect twelve hugs a day for the next week. Be aware of how your energy changes as a result of touch.

The Power of Beliefs

Our first lesson in this School of Love begins by identifying ancestral beliefs about self-love and loving others. Why? We all carry implicit beliefs in our unconscious mind which we inherited before we began kindergarten. Unless we inquire about our inherited, intergenerational beliefs, we behave as if our limited beliefs are true. Researchers estimate that 90% of our lives is directed from the unconscious level.

❖ To begin to identify some of your own intergenerational beliefs about self-loving and loving others, gather what you need to write or type and record your immediate responses to the following directions.

- Take a breath and imagine that you are your mother. The goal is to identify how your mother perceived her world in terms of self-loving and loving others. Using your intention and breath, softly say, "I am (your name), daughter/son of (mother's name) and I desire to examine my mother's beliefs about self-loving and loving others." Support yourself with your breath and when you have unearthed several beliefs, send out your thanks for the information and return to your normal state. Write down your mother's beliefs.

- Shift your body position to signal your unconscious that you are ready to access another ancestral voice. Using the same process as before, call in the beliefs of your maternal grandmother. Even if you do not know your grandmother, invite stories that you have heard about her.

- When you feel complete, once again shift to a different body posture and prepare to call on the energies of your maternal great-grandmother using the process outlined above. Record the many beliefs.

- Read out loud all the beliefs you have recorded and place an asterisk next to any beliefs that no longer serve you.

- Place a heart around the beliefs that promote self-loving.

- Next, identify beliefs about self-loving and loving others from your paternal ancestors, beginning with your father, moving to your grandfather, and ending with great-grandfather.

- Finally, list your personal beliefs about love and self-loving.
- Reflect on your lists. What beliefs feel true for you? Which beliefs are outdated and need to be released? What new beliefs do you wish to add to your life?

In order to reprogram your unconscious mind, I invite you to release any ancestral beliefs that are not aligned with love. You might wish to burn, bury, or flush them down the toilet. The physical action of making them vanish adds momentum.

Now it is time to plant more seeds of love into your unconscious. Be bold since your unconscious does not discern the difference between reality and fantasy. For instance, you might choose to adopt the following beliefs: "Love leads my life," or "Love is my protection," or "I choose loving awareness." Maintaining your focus on self-loving, please answer the following questions: In order to say yes to loving myself more:

❖ I will say yes to_____
❖ I will say no to_____

The next step in loving self is releasing yourself from blaming, shaming, and "shoulding." Whenever you overhear yourself saying, "I should," take a breath and ask yourself whose voice you are obeying. In order to end the ancestral trance of sabotaging love, you need to be aware of who planted the limiting belief. Then release the limiting belief and substitute the new love seed belief. See what happens when you substitute the words "I choose" in place of "I should."

Poet Mary Oliver summarizes the process of letting go of old beliefs that hold us back: "In order to be the person I want to be, I must strive hourly against the drag of others. It takes a tremendous amount of self-love to stay true to your path." The following exercise will begin to help you ground in self-love. Write down:

❖ What I loved about my life today was: _____. Then take a gentle breath and read your love list out loud or record it.
❖ What I loved about myself on this day includes_____ and fill the page with your positive emotions. Next take a gentle breath and read your love list out loud or record it. Remember to note the date.

Developing Love Muscles

When I committed to lead my life from the consciousness of "I am loving awareness" (thank you, Ram Dass), my capacity to both receive and give love skyrocketed. And I opened my heart to the planet and felt a renewed love for the earth, even the elves, fairies, and nature devas who reside here in the unseen dimensions. When I volunteer at my grandchildren's school, I put my hand on the backs of the students and call them "Love" and "Sweetheart," and they respond with smiles and sometimes with hugs.

Risk falling in love with the one inside you. As you blossom with self-love, you draw others to you like a magnet. Love is contagious in a positive way. Imagine that love has the power to transform neighborhoods, communities, politics, and even the world. Joan Chittister, author of *Seeing with Our Souls,* writes, "If you want to know if you love yourself enough, ask yourself how much time you take in a week to do what you love to do."

❖ Brainstorm your responses to the following question to discover new ways to love yourself: In what ways can I surround myself with self-love while loving others?

I have been a student of love for at least three decades. While writing this book, I reviewed my past journals and re-connected with the challenges of love and loving. Clearly, at times I pursued love. Upon reflection, I also realized that love pursued me. For example, I was asked to volunteer to teach a summer Bible school class for a week. Initially, I resisted the idea. Then I realized that collaborating with other adults was an invitation to love one hundred children I had never met before.

I know in my bones that love calls each of us to co-create our personal future as well as the future of our planet. Paul Ferrini, author of *Embracing Our True Self,* writes, "Once you have learned to love yourself in all your unruliness and complexity, with all of your contradictions, your ambivalence, your self-deceptions, once you have learned to love the dark side, the hidden lunar surface of your consciousness, the anger and sadness, the self judgment and feelings of powerlessness—you have mastered the hardest part of the curriculum." Love links us to the future. We become what we value. If we deeply value love, then love becomes our future. Without its energizing power, we remain in a mold dictated by our past hurts and fears.

One of my favorite stories about love is about Mahatma Gandhi. He spent much of his long imprisonment in solitary confinement. During most of his time in prison, he was allowed to receive mail only twice a year. Few visitors were permitted. Since he was deprived of human contact, he made a commitment to love each person who walked into his cell. He loved his torturers, his guards, and his doctors equally. His loving was so powerful that his guards were changed regularly because they became too sympathetic to the prisoner they were charged with controlling.

The Dance of Unconditional Loving and Thinking

Unconditional loving coexists with unconditional thinking. Unconditional love is an aspect of our consciousness. It is the energy that connects the body to the soul. Unconditional thinking is the partner of unconditional loving. It is the recognition of what is present without judging. Both aspects beckon us to become more whole. The first step toward the integration of the loving heart and the knowing mind is to love each aspect equally. Several times in my spiritual journey after I'd practiced unconditional loving for months, I was challenged to shift gears and wrap my heart around unconditional thinking.

Looking back, I fondly refer to these times as Life at the Crossroads. Each time I surrendered and embraced unconditional thinking, my understanding expanded. For example, I believed that our ancestors were relatives who had lived before us until the Elders at Taos Pueblo taught me about future ancestors. Each time the tribe faced an important decision, they invited the spirits of their past ancestors and their future ancestors to cast their votes. Each time I consider making an important decision, I imagine how my actions might affect my great, great, great-grandchildren.

Here is a journal entry about unconditional thinking in action:

I visited the grammar school at Taos Pueblo, in Taos, New Mexico today. Taos Pueblo is one of the oldest and longest inhabited Native American communities in the United States. Since I am a former teacher, I am fascinated with alternative teaching methods. I noticed that every time a child asked a question, the teacher replied, "Why don't you go outside and ask your question of the tree?" Another time she suggested, "How about going outside and asking your question of the river?" Still another time she directed the student to go outside and ask her question in the direction of sacred Blue Mountain.

As each child returned, grinning, the teacher inquired, "Did your question get answered?" Each student nodded. Then she asked, "Is there anything you wish to share with your family?"

Without exception each student described something unexpected and true.

I waited until lunchtime to ask the teacher how she knew where to send each child. She looked at me strangely and I wondered if she might decide to send me outside for my answer. Then she laughed.

"Oh, you think I know the magic spot for each child. Not so. My truth is no matter where I send them in Nature, the answer each receives will be a bigger answer than what I can offer. As long as they have open hearts and open minds, the sacred places will speak to and teach each of them."

Then I remembered how one of the girls told me, "Mommy Nature is wise." I smile in gratitude to the school children of the Taos Pueblo for reminding me of a new sense of intimacy with Mommy Earth.

Another opportunity to align my consciousness with unconditional thinking happened to me a few weeks after my father's death. I had tracked his energy in the afterlife for a couple of weeks without making a connection with his essence. However, on this occasion, he recognized my energy, and I heard him exclaim with my inner ears, "When did you learn how to do this?" followed abruptly by, "When did you stop being my little girl?" The power of our meeting still makes me cry and I continue to savor the experience. From spirit, my dad was finally able to behold me with unconditional thinking, and to see me as multidimensional.

More recently, unconditional love and thinking were absent from my consciousness and then my heart exploded as it witnessed a deeper truth. I was sitting in a middle row watching my grandson's basketball game. A large man with long, greasy, uncombed hair that hung below his shoulders ambled over from the other side of the gym. He was overweight and dressed like he was prepared to clean his barn.

My judgments crumbled when I watched as he picked up a young girl about five years old and swung her around, holding her securely. She giggled and I watched his face transform with love. He swung her around a couple more times. Her face lit up, and as I looked around, everyone's eyes were on the two of them. My heart opened. I do not know any more of their story. He was a powerful teacher for me.

Research tells us that an act of kindness affects not only the people giving and receiving the loving act, but also anyone who is watching or is in the energetic field. I believe the same principle is true about love. Love impacts us. Although I was not the one twirled around, I felt the power of love. I am reminded of a quotation I heard many years ago, by Meister Eckhardt, "Love has no why."

High Heart as Magnetic Compass

Your high heart is the energy center that is located midway between your human heart and your throat. It is the magnetic center of your multi-dimensional being and connects you with unlimited time-space. High heart is the bridge to your divine potential, the inner voice of your spirit. Some people refer to high heart as their all-knowing heart, or their spiritual heart. Think of it as your inner compass that connects you with your intuition and to your essence.

In order to reside in your high heart, you must discipline and still your mind. Once you become comfortable residing in your high heart, which is the deepest part of self, your soul begins to empower your intuition. When we awaken our high heart, we align with the God dimension within our self. Our life then takes on a sacred dimension. For me, essence is your sacred individuality. Hildegard, a mystic who lived in the twelfth century, stretches her voice across time and invites us to "listen with the ears of our heart." Why? Truth resonates in our heart and in every cell of our body. Mental understanding is not truth. Think of the heart's intelligence as loving truth.

❖ Here's a way to connect with high heart.
- Take a gentle breath and breathe into the spaciousness of your high heart.
- Remember a time when you felt deeply loving.
- Breathe love into your high heart and surround yourself with the frequency of love. Experience the expansiveness of your high heart.
- When you feel overflowing with love, I invite you to respond to the following:
- I can become even more centered in my high heart if___
  _____
- I know when I am making decisions that are not in alignment with my high heart when_____

- I know when my high heart is open because _____
  _____

Now close your eyes and experience letting go of every belief about self-love that does not resonate with the frequency of your high heart. It is essential to release inner obstacles to self-love in order to give and receive love. Move to your high heart, and you can shift from victim to creator.

Separation from Love

Leonard Laskow, author of *Healing with Love*, tells us, "Our difficulties with love often result from early childhood experiences or perceptions of betrayal, abandonment, humiliation, or rejection which lead to feelings of unworthiness, shame, and guilt." Pain always shows what is blocking you from the awareness of love. We often shield our hearts by acting out and repressing our emotions. Characteristics of a closed heart include:
- Difficulty trusting
- Blaming others for your pain
- Fear of being rejected
- Arguing to prove you are right
- Feeling easily hurt
- Lack of compassion for self and others
- Absence of gratitude
- Alienation from wonder and awe

Developing Love Muscles

Our hearts cannot be open and closed at the same time, just as love and fear cannot occupy the same space. Each time we give or receive love, we increase our connection to our high heart and our soul and decrease our sense of separation. Any time we close our heart, we are cutting off our access to the flow of love. It is no longer helpful to close our hearts down to create a boundary, to nurture a grudge, or to protect ourselves. Remember that love is our protection. It is not necessary to invite everyone in. It is only essential to remain open to the endless flow of love, inspiration, and grace.

Each time we close our hearts even a little, we eclipse our present as well as our future. To the degree that we shut our hearts down, our ego cheers and assumes even more control of our experience and our expression.

Ego is invested in power, not love, unless it is the love of power. The power of love is connected to our essence.

Love is the key to our authentic self. Love is the midwife. Love is the catalyst that moves us beyond ego to essence. The simple response to the chant "Keep Your Heart Open," which you will find in the Appendix, is "My Heart is Open." An open heart keeps the dimensional doorways open. My friend, Hiromi Dolliver, reminds me often, "When your heart is open, tears of joy flood you."

The choice to reside in the spaciousness of our high heart is the route to self-empowerment and soul empowerment. Spirit merges with our humanness through our heart. Spirit is connected to our life force, and it yearns for its own evolution through us. According to Alan Jones, author of *Soul Making: the Desert Way of Spirituality,* "Things of the spirit operate by different laws than those of the material world. Sharing diminishes material goods. Spiritual things like love, joy, peace are increased, not diminished when they are shared." When we lift our energies from our human heart to our high heart, we connect with our guides and teachers. Remember that they are in our energetic field to remind us of love. High heart is the seat of unconditional love as well as unconditional thinking. Positive emotions of hope, happiness, wonder, passion, and creativity can pour out when we are centered in high heart.

❖ Take a moment and breathe into your high heart to access your inner voice and wisdom. Close your eyes and take a deep breath.

- Write down the following question, "What does my heart want to tell me right now?"
- Using your non-dominant hand, begin to take dictation from your high heart. If you run out of words, breathe into your high heart and write, "thank you, thank you, thank you," until the words begin to reach you. Once again, use your non-dominant hand to record your high heart's wisdom.
- When you are finished, reflect on what you have written. Then lovingly read your guidance out loud.
- If you are willing, make a commitment to put the words of wisdom into action immediately. What is one thing you can do right now?

Truth is a frequency, and our souls respond to truth. High heart is the doorway to all that is. Yes, the high heart is the opening to loving, forgiving, and extending compassion to our selves. To move beyond ego and access soul empowerment, we need a motivator that is stronger than our embedded ego. Soul is that power, and it is connected to your high heart.

I challenge you to give a 51% vote to your high heart, the seat of your intuition. Let your heart direct the purpose of your life. Lou Ann Daly, author of *Humans Being,* reminds us, "Your heart knows your path. To the extent you are listening and following its wisdom, your body moves with ease to support you. In silence the answers are revealed."

Love as Motivator

Forty years ago Dr. Abraham Maslow, author of *The Further Reaches of Human Nature*, introduced a hierarchy of needs that included:
- Basic physiological needs: oxygen, water, sleep, sex, avoidance of pain
- Safety and security needs: stability, protection, and safe circumstances
- Love and belonging needs: affectionate relationships, friends, and community
- Esteem needs: respect of others, recognition, confidence, competence, independence, and freedom
- Self-actualization needs: the continuous desire to fulfill potential

Dr. Maslow believed that we all have basic needs that are genetically based. For example, if you are deprived of water, you feel a need to procure water. Once you satisfy your thirst, the basic need ceases to motivate you until another need gains your attention. Maslow made a distinction between survival needs, which he called deficiency needs and growth needs, which he called being needs.

❖ Let's take a closer look at love's motivation, depending on where we reside on Maslow's hierarchy of needs. Get ready to write your responses to the following questions. Add as many details as you remember for each answer. Remember, you are tracking the growth of your consciousness!
- Do you remember loving a person because you feared being alone?

- Do you remember loving someone because you wanted to feel protected?
- Do you remember loving someone because you needed to belong to someone?
- Do you remember loving someone because you wanted to be in control of her/him?

If you answered "yes" to any or all of the above questions, your love was motivated by a deficiency need according to Maslow. When love is a deficiency need, you become an extension of the one you love.

- Do you remember looking out at the horizon with a lover and seeing or feeling a collaborative vision to be of service to the world?

If you answered "yes" to this question, both you and your lover were motivated by a growth need according to Maslow.

Being dedicated to a higher purpose is evidence of love as a motivation at the self-actualizing level. Love expands and magnifies. Growth needs have transcended deficiency or fear needs. As we move toward self-actualization and beyond that to self-transcendence, love becomes a motivation for further enlightenment. Love at this level is grounded by an attitude of fulfillment and an overflowing motivation to share. This is a love that embraces rather than a love that is needy and dependent on another. Love at the self-actualization level seeks for a higher union and synthesis. Love feels as if it is part of a person's mission.

Loving more happens naturally. Love itself becomes a basic need and primary motivation. When a self-actualizing person does not fulfill the innate need to give and receive love, he or she can experience depression, alienation, and cynicism. Maslow wrote a letter to a friend months before he died, saying that his research suggested that if a person who was at the self-actualization level did not overflow with love, that individual would suffer with meta-pathologies.

One of the principles in this School of Love is that we do not progress on our path towards authentic self unless we are willing to serve others. Mother Teresa reminds us that love has to be put into action, and that action is service. Listen to a story of a moving example of awakening to service:

At times a crisis can provoke a personal as well as a collective awakening to love and service. My granddaughter, Malia, was seven years old when the earthquake struck Haiti. She cried as she watched pictures of thousands of homeless families on television, and she decided to take action and to make a difference. She researched how much money it cost to feed a family of four like hers and began to make a plan. Her goal was to raise $900 by asking 900 people to donate one dollar each. She reasoned that most people would have one dollar in change in their pockets, and she did not want to embarrass anyone by asking for too much. Her outreach project included e-mailing people, knocking on neighbors' doors, appealing to her classmates, enlisting the help of other Girl Scouts, and making an appeal at her church. Ordinarily, Malia does not seek out opportunities to speak in front of large groups, but her passion to make a difference propelled her to speak from her heart to help others. She was a girl with a mission. She created posters and made a donation box. Before the month's end, she had reached her goal and sent a $900 check to Doctors Without Borders.

Duane Elgin, author of *The Living Universe,* writes, "As we deepen our awareness, we find that love is our core essence at the very heart and center of our experience." In the thirteenth century, Rumi wrote, "Everything has to do with love and not loving." Fast forward almost seven centuries and listen to Marianne Williamson: "Everything can be interpreted as love or a call for love."

The Lessons of Trust

Trust is an important prerequisite for love. It has three dimensions: trusting self, trusting the process, and trusting the universe. Trust love to be as limitless as consciousness. Have you experienced your inner resistance reaching a peak when a breakthrough is imminent? Think of resistance as the province of ego, and observe how ego craves control.

❖ When faced with a challenge, breathe into the spaciousness of your high heart and track your inner responses to the following questions:
  • As a loving person, what is most important for me to remember at this moment?
  • What is the most loving response I can make? Is it true? Does it need to be said? Can it be said with kindness and love?

Trust yourself to know what feels like a high heart response. What is the hidden gift in this situation? Smile and express your gratitude for the opportunity to evolve your love capacity. Here is another true story about the expanding power of love.

I was driving near Oceanside, California, when I was ordered by a policeman to pull over and stop my car. A two-car accident blocked the freeway. I told the policeman that I was a minister and asked if he thought anyone involved in the car wreck needed to speak with me. He nodded and pointed to a man who was already surrounded by paramedics. I walked quickly over to him, sensing that there was little time. I introduced myself and asked him if he would like to pray.

"I'm dying," he whispered. "Not much time left."

I nodded, knowing he was right.

"I don't believe in God," he said. "You got any other suggestions?"

Without thinking, I said, "Do you believe in love?"

He nodded his head slightly and then said, "Yes."

"How about letting yourself remember all the times you loved this lifetime?"

He closed his eyes, and I was not sure if he was dead or alive. After a few minutes he squeezed my hand slightly and said, "Okay, what's next?"

Since I had never done this before, I breathed into my high heart and asked. The response I heard was, "Now remember all the times people loved you."

Again he nodded, closed his eyes and I continued to send love to him. He surprised me by opening his eyes and saying, "You know, I am beginning to believe that maybe there is a God."

I moved close to his ear and whispered, "God bless you and your journey."

I do not know if he heard me, and it really didn't matter because he had died surrounded by love. I stayed with him for another few minutes before I turned his body over to others. Before I returned to my car, I realized I did not even know his name. How strange to interact with someone's soul without even knowing his name!

Love's Call to Surrender

Remember that to let love in requires a decision to melt. Why? Whenever we invite love to have its way with us, it will challenge any beliefs, feelings, and experiences that exist outside its circumference. Pause for a moment and ask your inner guidance, "What new capacities do I need to develop in order to continue to be aware of love?" Listen to the words of Martha Lunney, a heart-centered friend who e-mailed this message telling me how her heart opened unexpectedly on an ordinary day:

"Some time ago, I was riding the bus between my job and my private practice office and, looking around at the range of faces from all circumstances of life there on the bus, I had the simple epiphany that if I really let in that each of these people on the bus had hopes and dreams and their own lives, my heart would break open. It was something like being poised right on the edge of heartbreak and heart breaking open."

Forgiveness as Teacher

Remember also that in this School of Love, our capacity to understand, forgive, and accept is directly linked to our personal health. The ancient Greek word for forgiveness is *aphesis* which means to let go. Listen to Mark Twain's definition of forgiveness: "Forgiveness is the fragrance that the violet sheds on the heel that has crushed it." When we forgive others, we release our judgments as well as our attachments to the story we tell ourselves that reinforces our grudge. Challenge your judgments by asking yourself: What is the story I am telling myself in order to hold on to my grudge?

Mastering the power of forgiveness is essential to your spiritual path of love. Forgiveness is a conscious choice to cultivate love and let go of judgments. Compassion precedes forgiveness. We choose to forgive because we feel compassion for others and ourselves.

Forgiveness releases the pain of the past from your heart. Heart-centered forgiveness extends in three directions: forgiveness from the person you hurt, forgiveness for yourself and forgiveness for those who have hurt you.

Forgiveness in Action

Love honors the sacredness of the soul. Lack of forgiveness blocks the flow of energy. When your inner sense of the sacred feels compromised, I recommend the following three-step process, proposed by James R. Jones, author of *Transformational Practices Group Guide*:

- I Forgive: my own judgments, words, actions, as well as the actions and reactions of others.
- I Bless: directed to self or other.

- I Release: remove the incident from your consciousness and from your relationship.

Forgiveness frees up energy for loving and healing. It does not change the injury that happened in the past, but it does free you to step into your future. You will know you have forgiven someone when you see the person upon whom you have projected your judgments and recognize that you no longer have a negative emotional reaction.

A Forgiveness Practice

Jeanne Acterberg, Barbara Dossey, and Leslie Kolkmeier, co-authors of *Rituals of Healing,* recommend the following six-step forgiveness ritual:

- Taking responsibility for what you have done
- Confessing the nature of the wrong to yourself, another human being, or God
- Looking for the good points
- Being willing to make amends where possible, as long as you can do this without harm to yourself or other people
- Looking to God for help
- Inquiring about what you have learned

Here is my personal story about the far-reaching effects of forgiveness:

I was bitten by a brown recluse spider. It was serious. The previous week, a man had died from a similar bite. I did not see the spider. I didn't even know I was bitten until my forearm swelled and turned red. The hard, round red spot on my left upper arm ached. I labeled myself a whiny wimp and continued to participate in my belly dancing class in the morning and my interfaith ministry class in Santa Fe.

When I could no longer move my left arm, I consulted a doctor. He shook his head gravely and said there was no cure. The only thing he recommended was a homeopathic remedy made up of the venom of killer bees.

As I prepared to leave, he almost whispered that he knew a "curandera," a local Hispanic medicine woman who lived close to me. He called her and drove me to her house. My fever was high and I wondered if I could be hallucinating.

The elderly woman, who spoke no English, helped me undress and pointed to a bed in front of a hot wood stove. She pulled out an ancient looking rattle from her travel bag and returned to the stove to brew some herbs that would take the fire out of my fever.

She spoke to me in Spanish, and I understood a few words. The doctor translated, "I will stay awake at the bottom of this bed until you are ready to come back from the center of the universe. I will rattle and sing your spirit to remind you of here."

For hours I traveled in and out, hot and cold, moaning and crying. I traversed the spaces between living and dying, choosing neither. I wondered if this was karmic, to be part of nothing. Three days passed. Always I was aware of the rattling song. As I watched my life before me, I could not say, "Well done" about three incidents in my life story. I cried as I felt both the pain I had caused and the pain I had endured by refusing to forgive. My heart beat fast and I could feel it wanting to open more. I cried, wishing I could return and have a second chance to let go of my pride and surrender by forgiving and being forgiven. Suddenly I realized I could return and heal those relationships. The choice was mine, and I was determined to return and master forgiveness.

The Co-Arising of Stress and Love

Learning how to utilize stress is an essential skill in our School of Love because love often disappears when stress visits. Look at your beliefs about stress. What do you believe your mind/body is capable of? Each of us programs our individual stress response from earlier life experiences. We all have both a child brain, which is helpless and fearful, and an adult brain, which is capable, optimistic, and able to solve problems. When fear takes over, your child brain takes charge of your reactions. Fears and stress quickly translate into muscular tension.

We create more stress when we perceive that we are not enough or do not have enough inner and outer resources to handle the emerging situation. "It is not the potential stressor but how we perceive it and then how we handle it that will determine whether or not it will lead to stress," concluded Dr. Martin Seligman, author of *Learned Optimism,* from his research on optimism and health.

According to Brian Luke Seaward, 80% of illness and disease is caused by stress, but too few do anything about it. Landmark long-term studies conducted by Dr. Hans Eysenck and colleagues at the University of London have shown that chronic unmanaged stress is as much as six times more predictive of cancer and heart disease than cigarette smoking, cholesterol level, or blood pressure, and much more responsive to intervention.

A certain amount of stress is necessary for growth and change. "Stress is the glue that holds us together sometimes," Nancy Long, a nurse at Eastern Maine Medical Center, said to me as I waited for my daughter to come back from surgery. Dr. Norman Shealy, author of *Soul Medicine,* points out, "It is not stress itself but the reaction to stress or the feeling that stress is uncontrollable that makes stress harmful."

Stress even interferes with our ability to learn. Recently researchers at the University of California in San Francisco discovered that lab rats having a new experience did not absorb it into their memories until they had a break from their activity. Without downtime that allows the brain to relax and absorb what's new, the research suggests that learning suffers, fatigue mounts, and creativity stalls. Trying to stay engaged and active every single minute backfires. Simple daydreaming for 10 to 15 minutes works.

The antidote for the stress response is the love response, which is made from one part awareness, one part breath, and one part self-honoring. The act of loving induces a relaxation response that releases oxytocin and dopamine and resembles the biochemical qualities of a meditative response.

Stress and love coexist, just as fear and love coexist. We are always at a choice point. Stress compromises our immune system and tends to enhance negative emotions and reactions. Love, in contrast, evokes the relaxation response and attracts positive emotions. Dr. Eva Selhub, author of *The Love Response*, reminds us that, "Love has the capacity to reestablish our balance and flow." Self-love is the key to our sense of inner resilience.

In order to return to your knowing heart during a stressful encounter, admit to yourself that you are in the midst of a stressful situation. Honor your experience without adding more stress by "shoulding" and shaming yourself. Next, take a gentle breath. Since you hold your breath when you respond to stress, intentional breathing reverses the stress response. Then remind yourself that your stress response is natural. Next, use your will and intention to remember one time when you felt overflowing with love. Remember the time with all of your senses. When you feel grounded in the remembered love honoring experience, breathe the loving energies into your high heart. Coming home to your heart when stress attacks is one of the lessons in the School of Love.

Toning Your Love Muscles

David Spangler, author of *Everyday Miracles,* suggests the following activity to stretch and tone your love muscles. Attune to a felt sense of love within yourself. Then imagine and feel this love flowing from your high heart into your arms and down into your hands and fingers. Imagine the loving energy collecting and radiating around your fingers. Whatever you touch, do so in the spirit of this lovingness, as if you are touching the most loved thing in the world. Imagine this loving, blessing energy flowing into and filling a sphere of energy surrounding you at arm's length or just a little further out. This sphere does touch everything; it engages with the subtle energies of the environment around you and, like your fingers, it too can convey the power and intent of your love.

Love Welcomes All

Another required course in the School of Love is to love everyone and every event that you encounter. This is a huge challenge at first. I continue to challenge myself by asking, "What is the most loving response I can make in this situation?" When I really feel at a loss for a loving response or perspective, I imagine how God might see it or be with it.

Love honors the sacredness of the soul. By taking responsibility for attracting every single person and event in our life, we grow in self-love and understanding. Take to heart the Attraction Principle, which invites us to reflect on our present relationships in order to design our own report card on how well we are progressing. Every relationship is a reflection of your love for yourself. We each attract people and events that mirror our self-love or our denial of self-love. Marianne Williamson, author of *A Return to Love*, reminds us that "Whenever you feel unloved, take it as a sign that you are disconnected from your heart. When we forget we are love, we forget to love."

In *Coming Back to Life*, Joanna Macy offers an exercise about cherishing a stranger as if he or she were a beloved parent from a previous lifetime in order to remind us of the power of love. I committed myself to practice her strategy. An hour later, as I was eating breakfast, I overheard an elderly man say to the waitress, "I'll join this lady," and he pointed directly to me.

I smiled to myself, marveling at the speed that turned my intention into reality. He sat down at my table and told me about the death of his wife and how his world had changed. He spoke about moving in with his fifth son and leaving his childhood friends. He also told me about his long days and endless nights. When I asked him what he enjoyed doing he said, "Fishing, but I can't walk very steadily since my hip replacement surgery." He also said he used to play the banjo but his hands were crippled with arthritis.

I listened with my open heart and reached out and held his hands. We both cried. Then he said he hoped his wife did not hate him for abandoning her in the nursing home. He could not bear to see her in pain. Then he whispered, "You know we always talked about me dying first. Never did I dream she would leave me behind." I smiled and patted his wrinkled hands. We were both silent for a few minutes. Then he said, "You know, I just realized that she was the one who abandoned me and I know that will make a big difference in the way I get up every morning."

Listening to him and loving him was easy since he was about the same age as my own father. If only I could be in relationship with everyone I met in a cherishing way, I know my soul would be happy. Before we finished breakfast, I invited him to swim with me and he said he might "someday."

When the waitress brought our checks, he reached for them saying, "Let me pay for your breakfast. You have been a loving companion this morning." I smiled as tears filled my eyes. When I moved over to hug him goodbye, I noticed he had tears in his eyes too. I returned to my car appreciating how naturally love, compassion, and forgiveness connect us to ourselves and each other. When we love from our souls, loving transforms into a way of being.

Love is connected to our souls, and it is our souls that radiate our inner light. Once you align with your knowing heart, you begin to feel an inner fulfillment, and the human tendency to project our emptiness on others fades. Dawna Markova, author of *I Will not Die an Unlived Life*, speaks from her heart when she writes, "We grow stronger in the fact of loving something. It sustains us. It generates energy. If I am depleted or feel as if I've failed, ultimately it is because I have not been living in service to what I love."

I invite all of you to send love to a couple of people a day. You can do this practice as you stand in line at a grocery store or when you are waiting for the light to turn green. Surround a stranger with love. Appreciate that each time we extend love, we are blessing. Experience how your life transforms when you treat someone else with love.

The Frequency of Love

Love is high frequency energy. According to Gary Zukov, author of *The Seat of the Soul*, "Love and trust produce positive emotions such as gratitude, contentment, and joy." Other high frequency energies include courage, generosity, happiness, and forgiveness. The experience and expression of positive feelings have far reaching benefits that include:

- A relaxed and calm physical body
- A stronger immune system
- A cardio-vascular system that is a buffer against stress
- Healthy relationships
- A quiet mind
- Increased optimism
- Deepened resilience

As I was finishing this chapter, I remembered a chant I had learned more than 30 years ago. I felt like the chant reached across time and reclaimed me. Although I have sung it many times during my lifetime, I never embraced it as a song about self-love. I offer the song to you in the spirit of loving yourself. "Listen, listen, listen to my heart's song, I will never forget you, I will never forsake you, Listen, listen, listen to my heart's song."

Embracing and embodying self-love means I no longer rely on external connections to make me feel good or fill me up. Self-loving means I honor myself and my unique rhythms and cycles. As I grow in self-love, I have more love to offer others as well as the world. Consider that your whole life is a test of love. The only question on your final examinations is: How much and how well did I love? Keeping your heart open is an act of self-love that honors your soul. This is a sacred alignment. The all-knowing heart feels safe and resilient when it is filled with self-love. Intuition is the voice that overflows from a loving heart.

The following two offerings read like a duet. Treat yourself to this loving benediction by Fyodor Dostoevsky, author of *Crime and Punishment*:

"Love all God's creation, the whole and every grain of sand in it. Love every leaf, every ray of God's light: love the animals, love the plants, love everything. If you love everything, you will perceive the divine mystery in things. Once you perceive it, you will begin to comprehend it better every day. And you will come at last to love the whole world with an all-embracing love." And Terri St. Cloud's response:

Slowly, she was beginning to see it,

28

It wasn't about acting or thinking or getting or giving love.
It was about breathing love-
Becoming love.

Reflective Love Questions

- How have you answered love's call this day?
- If you believed that love is all that mattered, how would your life be different?
- Name your love teachers this lifetime.
- What opens your heart?
- If you believed that love is all that mattered, how would you lead your life differently?
- When are you most loving of yourself? What brings you joy?
- What is your capacity for love?

Awakening Reflection Responses

In *Harvesting Your Journals: Writing Tools to Enhance Your Growth and Creativity*, Alison Strickland and I challenged ourselves and our readers to respond to the following questions after bundling our journal entries together into themes. I invite you to reflect on the Love chapter and record your insights for this day.

- ❖ I Learned_____
- ❖ I Relearned_____
- ❖ I Discovered_____
- ❖ I Rediscovered_____
- ❖ I Regret_____
- ❖ I Appreciate_____
- ❖ Right Now I Feel_____
- ❖ And I Will_____

Journaling Prompts

Here are a few prompts to give you more to wrap your all-knowing heart around. Feel free to agree, disagree, make your own connections, or write your own quotations.

"Love is the way I walk in gratitude." *Course in Miracles*

"Love and coercion can never go together, but while love cannot be forced upon anyone, it can be awakened by love itself. Those who do not have it catch it from those who have it. It goes on gathering power and spreading itself until eventually it transforms everyone it touches. Humanity will attain a new mode of being and lift itself through the free and unhampered interplay of pure love from heart to heart." Meher Baba

"Love is the continuous birth of creativity within and between us." John O'Donahue

"In a full heart, there is room for everything and in an empty heart there is room for nothing." Antonio Ponchia

"There is no difficulty that enough love will not conquer, no disease that enough love will not heal, no door that enough love will not open, no gulf that enough love will not bridge, no wall that enough love will not throw down, no sin that enough love will not redeem." Emmet Fox

If we are to offer peace and healing to the world, we must begin in our own hearts. I invite you to reside in the spaciousness of your high heart as you explore the rich connections between love and emotions in the next chapter.

Chapter Two

Emotions

Emotions as Teacher

"A life that is truly lived is constantly burning away the veils of illusions, gradually revealing the essence of the individual."
- Marion Woodman

As I was revising this chapter for the fourth and final time, I e-mailed my friend Alison, "I am done with emotions." We both laughed. Feeling our feelings is part of being human. I remember telling clients to think of feelings as keys on a piano where each note added its tone to our songs of self. In order to move beyond ego, we must be willing to experience and express our feelings. Emotional integrity is part of empowerment.

Self-regulating our emotions is an essential skill when we commit to growing our consciousness. Emotion is the source of power that drives us forward towards our goals in life. Unless we commit ourselves to emotional self-care, our emotions will rule, confuse, deceive, and sabotage our best intentions. According to Leonard Laskow, author of *Healing with Love*, "The feeling response to life is the slowest one to change in transformation." You are probably already aware that once an emotion is experienced, it becomes a powerful motivator of future behaviors, affecting moment-to-moment actions, attitudes, and long-term achievements.

We all have the inner resources and freedom to create new neuro-networks in our brains that resonate with emotional self-care. You can learn to identify, experience, and express your feelings so that you remain true to yourself. Alan Cohen, author of *The Dragon Doesn't Live Here*

Anymore, reminds us that our emotional body does not really care what it feels. It enjoys stimulation of any kind. In fact, it will feel nourished through joy, sorrow, exuberance, anger, surprise, disappointment, and even fear.

The Biology of Emotions

The Institute for HeartMath has found a critical link between the heart and the emotions. As we experience emotional reactions like anger, frustration, anxiety, and insecurity, heart rhythms become incoherent or jagged, interfering with the communication between the heart and the brain. Negative emotions create a chain reaction in the body. Blood vessels constrict, blood pressure rises, and the immune system weakens. This kind of consistent imbalance puts a strain on the heart and other organs and eventually leads to serious health problems. On the other hand, when we experience heart-felt emotions such as love, caring, appreciation, and compassion, the heart produces smooth, coherent rhythms that enhance communication between the heart and the brain. Positive emotions produce harmonious rhythms that are connected to cardiovascular efficiency, a relaxed, balanced nervous system, enhanced immunity, and hormonal balance.

The Speed of Emotions

Emotions spread so rapidly that your happiness can affect not just your children, spouse, and close friends, but 258 people in a single day. According to Christakis and Fowler, every time you feel an emotion—whether it is hope or anger, gratitude or fear—it spreads to six people you know: family and friends, neighbors and coworkers. Then it spreads again to six people each of them knows, and *again*, to 6 people each of *those* people know. By the end of the day, your emotion has touched 258 others.

The Frequency of Emotions

Begin to relate to each of your thoughts and feelings as a frequency tuning fork. Frequency serves as an attractor just like a magnet. We create our reality by the frequency and repetitiveness of our thoughts. Notice how each of your thoughts and feelings have a high or low energetic frequency. For example, love has a high frequency, while jealousy has a low frequency. The statement, "I am a creator," carries a high frequency, while the statement, "I am a failure," carries a low energetic frequency. Feelings and beliefs about lack and scarcity vibrate at a low frequency, while abundance and optimism register at a high frequency. Withholding and withdrawing your love creates a profound separation from your essence and vibrates at a low frequency. Resisting love is a low frequency that holds you back in the School of Love. If the feeling does not feel like love, it probably comes from fear. Unresolved emotions, no matter how old, cloud the present moment and compromise our capacity to love ourselves and others. Dr. Carl Jung, author of *The Undiscovered Self*, called emotions the chief source of consciousness. He wrote, "There is no change from darkness to light or from inertia to movement without emotion." The most efficient way to change our thoughts and mental patterns is to engage our will to deal with emotional wounds quickly before they scab over and negatively affect our present day beliefs.

❖ Here is a strategy to use when you choose to mobilize your will:

- Imagine that you are standing in front of a locked, closed door. On a scale of 1-10, how do you feel right now? If you rated yourself as low on that scale, consider that your emotions are vibrating at a low frequency and you are probably focusing on the problem and not the solution.
- Take a gentle breath, breathe into your high heart, and make a conscious choice to step away from the locked door and check out the open doors that surround you.
- Imagine the possibilities you could discover in each open room.
- Be aware of how the frequency of your emotion changes as you stand before the open door.

Listen to a true story from one of my journals that describes the impact of repressed emotions—even after many lifetimes. In case you are unfamiliar with the role of a balian, it is similar to a Native American medicine man or woman. A balian is on call 24 hours a day to serve people in their healing journeys. No one is turned away.

"I will not let you be harmed this lifetime," said the petite Balinese woman healer standing next to me. We were about to participate in a sacred ritual. Then my vision blurred. I halted in mid-step as the balian continued to climb up the steep stone steps that led to the priest and the high altar. I understood the man dressed in the long gold robe at the top of the stairs was waiting for me. I knew he was responsible for creating the life-affirming ritual. Yet I was overwhelmed by panic.

I tried to banish my fear by staring into the eyes of the priest, but I was filled with a nauseating sense of injustice.

"I will not let anyone harm you again. I will protect you," the balian said through the translator.

I wanted to scratch her face or throw her down the stairs. I was shocked by my reaction to the loving, peaceful woman who was my teacher and friend. Then I began remembering more details of the past lifetime. I was a teenage virgin. Nothing prepared me for the acrid smells of the scorching fire and the heavy blindfold that blocked my vision. I shuddered when I remembered how the heat of the fire burned my nostrils. My last body memory was my terrified screams as my young body disappeared in the flames.

The balian squeezed my hand more tightly. Instinctively, I recoiled from her touch. My body remembered how she was the one who had walked me to my death. As if reading my thoughts, she said loudly, "We are together again to heal. I will not allow you to be sacrificed ever again."

I searched her face for truth and reassurance. Smells of the past life story consumed me as I struggled to breathe. I remembered more. We were daughter and mother. She insisted on walking me to the fiery altar instead of allowing a paid guard to escort me to my death. Fascinated, I continued to watch the movie in my mind/body as she tried to jump in the pyre after me. I understood that it was all ordained from the moment I was born. I was the only one who had not known about my fate.

I grabbed for the balian's nearest hand. She pushed me forward as the elderly priest stepped towards us. I glanced around, frantically trying to orient myself in present time. He offered me a thin silver ring with two round black stones. The simple ring sealed my commitment to embody the energies of joy and compassion.

Then he intoned, "I dedicate your life to expanding the energies of joy and compassion. It is now and forever your duty to greet each moment and each person as an opportunity to spread compassion and joy."

He touched the top of my head, followed by my forehead and then my heart. Then he surprised me with an invitation to perform my soul's dance to honor the gods.

For a few seconds, I felt self-conscious and very young. Then I remembered to breathe. More recent memories surfaced. At that moment, I knew the reason I had traveled half way across the world to Bali was to integrate the long-buried emotional memories of sacrifice and the healing powers of sacred dance. I reminded myself I had studied Balinese dance for four weeks. However, I intuitively knew that my dance of dedication must be my unique dance. Hesitantly I moved my right arm and my left foot. The loud gamelan music spurred me from inside, and I began to spiral in harmonious movements. I did not plan the steps or movements; I simply wanted the dance to emerge from my heart. I hoped I spread delight as I flirted with the gods.

I wish someone had given me this quotation from Brugh Joy, author of *Joy's Way*, years ago: "Transformation enlarges the context of reality. The awareness is lifted into a state of consciousness where the multi-dimensional nature of existence is perceived, not just conceived, where it is experienced, not just imagined, where each dogma and each absolute truth is seen as but a single facet of a super conscious whole called Beingness." If someone had pointed out to me that many of my early experiences with energy were connected to transformation, I would have felt more confident and less alone.

Emotional Wounds

Feelings repressed in childhood retain their potency and influence our behavior. Any time a person or an event provokes upsetting emotions, it is important to be on the lookout for unexamined emotional wounds. Often when we are afraid, we are re-living the distant past. Virginia Satir, author of *Peoplemaking* and one of my favorite mentors, cautioned me to notice when my emotional reaction lasted longer than one minute. She was convinced that any emotional reaction that lasted more than sixty seconds was usually connected to lingering unfinished business.

Eventually self-awareness will uncover old emotional wounds. According to Frank Stainetti, author of *Awakening to the Miracle of Soul Merging*, the seven core wounds of humanity are fear, conditional love, rejection, separation, distrust, judgment, and death.

Pain, whether mental, emotional, or spiritual, is a resistance to your soul's purpose. Remember that pain is physical, and suffering is mental. Emotional pain results from clinging to old beliefs, old feelings, old identities, old wounds, and old grudges. If you choose not to acknowledge your painful emotions, pain will become suffering. Suffering is the result of wanting people or circumstances to be different from what they are. Clinging to a person, role, or cherished belief and resisting feeling and expressing your emotions increases suffering. It is important to identify what you are attached to in order to alleviate suffering.

Believe it or not, when your thinking changes, your pain also changes. Before your unexpressed pain deepens into bitterness and resentment, stop what you are doing and identify what meaning you have attached to the person or the event. For example, I used to be attached to being a perfect daughter. Each time I failed to meet my parents' expectations, which was often, I felt shame. When I realized that being a good enough daughter was more than enough, I felt free. The choice is always yours. You can continue to cling to your attachment and suffer, or you can relinquish the attachment and end the suffering. The question becomes, "How much pain are you willing to endure before you relinquish your attachment?" This short sentence from Deborah L. Johnson, author of *Your Deepest Intent: Letters from the Infinite,* offers a perfect summary of the dynamic between pain and future possibilities: "Pain pushes until vision pulls."

We create guilt when we hold on to the pain, unable to forgive ourselves for the role we played in its creation. Our judgmental voice lives inside our heads and convinces us that we did something wrong. Dwell in your all-knowing heart as you read this journal entry that illustrates the poisonous power of guilt and the healing power of love that allows letting guilt go.

A man called for a soul reading, saying, "I killed my father. Will you still see me for a soul reading?" His voice sounded weighed down with grief, urgency, and shame. I hesitated for a moment, trying to wrap my mind around what he had just said to me.

"I'll understand if you don't want to see me. What I did was a terrible and unforgivable thing, but I am searching for a reason to continue living, and a friend told me you do soul readings and talk to dead people. You are my last chance."

I explained to him that I could not guarantee that I could contact or channel his father, and I agreed to meet him.

"But I was told you see the big picture," he continued.

"Yes, I do. But I am not in charge of what I see. In the work I do, energy follows need. Clearly, you have a need for information. And perhaps your father has information and is capable of conveying information to you. I don't know if he is willing or capable of doing that. I wish I could promise you that I could channel his soul, but I don't want to raise your hopes and then disappoint you."

"What do I have to lose?" he asked in a flat voice.

"Only a few hours of your time," I replied candidly.

We met for a consultation a few days later. When I tuned in to his soul through his high heart, it was if I was taken over, and I spoke out loud in a deep, unfamiliar masculine voice, "Thanks for the boost, Son." No doubt his dad's energy was present.

Through me, his father explained that he had been diagnosed with terminal cancer and had not told anyone because he did not want pity or to be a burden. He said he thought about suicide and did not have the guts. He asked his son to remember how he had discovered the folder in the top desk drawer the day after the shooting. Then he described the numerous documents, will, insurance policy, deeds, and a stock brokerage deal that was dated the day before his death.

Dad continued, "I knew I was going to die. I did not know how. I knew cancer would not get me. When we agreed to go hunting, I knew I would not return alive. I did not know that you would trip and the gun would go off and I would die. Thank you, Son. You gave me the boost I prayed for and needed."

Norm's sobs filled the room. I, too, was crying. I was in awe of the story that was unfolding. From a human perspective, the son had endured a living hell because of a hunting "accident." Yet from a soul perspective, he had assisted his father in making a transition that his dad desired but did not dare to make on his own. There were no victims. Both father and son had played their parts perfectly.

The Freedom of Feeling

According to the Buddha, there are three kinds of feelings: pleasant, unpleasant, and neutral. All three have roots in the perceptions of mind and body. Centuries ago he counseled his followers to seek out the source of their upsetting emotions because all feelings are impermanent. He believed that almost all painful feelings have their source in an incorrect way of looking at reality. When you uproot erroneous views, suffering ceases.

Allow yourself to feel what you are feeling fully. Express your feelings to avoid a build up of emotional toxins in your body. Remember that if you choose to deny or block your emotions, you constrict your blood flow and deprive your organs of vital nourishment. Each time you choose to numb feelings, you numb yourself. Avoid emulating Woody Allen who declared, "I don't get depressed. I grow a tumor instead."

Fear is like a shadowy force hiding under our excuses, criticism, need to control, worry, and feelings of emptiness. We need to remember that it is words, concepts, and beliefs that keep us afraid. Many of our daily fears are based on anticipating shame, hurt, uneasiness, emptiness, sadness, or grief. When someone causes a strong emotional reaction that does not make sense in the present moment, take a deep breath and begin to ask creative questions, such as:

- What unconscious aspect of my personality is this person mirroring for me?
- Is this person bringing up a prior emotionally charged experience that I have buried?
- When have I felt this feeling in the past?

Fear diminishes your personal power and alienates you from your soul as well as your relationships. Remember that fear is a biological response. It also produces painful emotions such as anger, jealousy, grief, and vengefulness. Fear is a reaction to perceived danger and often manifests itself by momentary freezing or feeling stunned. Since fear is a conditioned reaction, it is usually attached to a younger aspect of yourself. Ask yourself, if your greatest fear happened, then what? Keep repeating "then what?" until you can laugh at yourself.

The common universal fears include:

- Fear of abandonment
- Fear of not being enough
- Fear of the unknown
- Fear of the future

Instead of being controlled by fear, remind yourself that you have the inner resources to create new neuro-networks in your brain when you shift to the love response and emotional self-care instead of the stress response. Once created, each time you do that, they grow stronger and expand.

- ❖ Take a few gentle breaths, adopt a friendly, inquiring attitude, and breathe into your high heart. When you feel centered in your heart, ask:
  - What fears continue to control me?
  - What events or people trigger my fear-based reaction?

- In what situations do I allow my fears to keep me small and contracted?

As the brain is to intelligence, so the heart is to emotional intelligence. Feeling will inform you. Emotions are always driven by a concern. We fuel our thoughts through emotion. In fact, emotions unite the mind and the body. Have you noticed that your most pervasive thoughts are typically fueled by the greatest intensity of emotion? Abraham Maslow, author of *The Farther Reaches of Human Nature,* warns us, "Anyone who tells me my emotions or desires don't exist is, in effect, telling me I don't exist!"

Research on Feelings

According to researchers at the Institute of HeartMath, while most of the adult population reports experiencing personal or emotional problems in the course of a year, about 50% of these people say they are unable to solve their problems, and about one third state they are unable to do anything to make their problems bearable. Heart rate variability or heart rhythms stand out as the most dynamic and reflective factors of inner emotional states and stress. According to HeartMath, intervening at the emotional level is the most efficient way to initiate change in mental patterns and processes.

Recent research proves that human emotion has a direct influence on the way our cells function in our body. During the 1990s, scientists working with the U.S. Army investigated to see if it was possible that the power of our feelings continues to have an effect on living cells, specifically DNA, once those cells are no longer part of the body. The researchers collected a swab of tissue and DNA from the inside of a volunteer's mouth, and the sample was taken to another room in the same building. The DNA was measured electrically to see if it responded to the emotions of the donor, who was in another room several hundred feet away.

Then the DNA donor viewed a series of video images that included graphic wartime footage, erotic images, and comedy. The goal was for the donor to experience a spectrum of real emotions within a brief period of time. While he was doing so, his DNA was measured in another room for its response.

The effect was instantaneous in each experiment, whether the cells were in the same room or separated by hundreds of miles. When the donor had an emotional experience, the DNA reacted as if it were still connected to the donor's body. As Dr. Jeffrey Thompson states, "There is no place where one's body actually ends."

Anger Spells Attachment

Where in your life are you angry or shame bound? Anger is projected out. Shame is turned inward. The core cause of anger is a lack of self-worth. Anger arises when you are hurt, in pain, afraid, or when something that you value has been violated. Often anger is based on our limited ideas of what should happen. Maharaj-ji tells us, "You can get angry with someone as long as you don't throw him or her out of your heart." In what ways would your life be different if you followed his advice?

The strength of your anger reveals the amount of your attachment. I am sensitive to being overlooked or unappreciated. Although I have worked hard to transform my core vulnerability, I still have to acknowledge that it is the pull of my past that is the trigger for my reactive anger when I feel judged, misunderstood, or overlooked. A time-tested strategy I use often is to remind myself to breathe before I speak. This pause results in more patience, gratitude, and respect for others. If breath does not release me from my attachment, I repeat "God is…" and fill in the blank until I resonate with a different perspective.

Although more than fifteen years have passed, I still remember the judgment I felt when my friend Mary Rae Means and I flew to a Crone's Conference in Arizona. We had created a business called Ripe Tomatoes that specialized in greeting cards designed especially for women who were approaching or in the throes of menopause. We thought the Crone Conference was the perfect venue to showcase our cards. I was caught completely off guard when the coordinator of the conference dismissed me and our creative cards proclaiming, "Obviously you are too happy to have allowed life to affect you." I admit some of the cards required a sense of humor, though others were serious. Her judgment infuriated me and reopened past wounds. Fortunately, I caught on to my programmed emotional outburst when I realized I had been ranting for more than five minutes. In order to transform any emotion, you must feel your feelings fully. When you discipline yourself to take a breath and evaluate each situation from a place of knowing heart, you will prevent yourself from overreacting.

Strong emotions are perfect teachers. Our challenge becomes how to discharge or transform powerful emotions that we might prefer to judge or deny. Curiosity counteracts judgment. Experiment with adopting a curious attitude to guard against labeling or judging "unacceptable" emotions as "The Enemy," and notice what happens.

The Negativity Nemesis

A negative attitude creates a negative response within your physical body. Solid research shows that every thought, feeling, mood, desire, and experience is accompanied by corresponding and instantaneous changes in our brain and our body. Furthermore, studies cited in *The Physiological Journal of Advanced Medicine* show that negative emotions can influence as many as 1,400 biochemical changes in the body including hormonal imbalance, heart rhythm chaos, mental fogginess, and poor performance.

Each time you judge an emotion as negative, you will find yourself defending, denying, or aggrandizing your emotional response. Resentment further anchors us in negativity without changing our reality. Dr. Candace Pert tells us that research suggests that hostility, anxiety, and other negative emotions deplete the immune system, leaving an individual vulnerable to disease.

Marci Shimoff advises that when you are plagued by a persistent negative thought, substitute an equally positive thought about the same situation. She suggests repeating the advice of the Zen masters who pray: "Thank you for everything. I have no complaints."

We all inherited survival instincts and strategies from our ancient ancestors. Our bodies and brains are on the lookout for danger. Did you know that, in terms of brain research, it is the negative experiences rather than the positive ones that have the most impact on survival? Rick Hanson, co-author of *Buddha's Brain*, explains that our brain is like Velcro for negative experiences and Teflon for positive ones. Our brain has a built-in negative bias left over from eons ago when staying constantly alert for signs of danger assured survival. Let down your guard and a tiger could jump you. When we're conscious of the bias passed down by our ancient ancestors, we can change our brains by purposefully confronting our fears and focusing on the many positive things we experience every day.

Strategies for Letting Go

Heed the words of Thich Nhat Hahn, author or of *The Precise Moment*, who advises us to practice taking good care of our anger, fear, confusion, and shame. He invites us to be like a good mother and embrace our strong emotions like a mother hugs a child. When we welcome and recognize emotions that we have judged as negative, we decrease their energetic charge, much like turning the volume down on a television set.

Remember that all emotions are a combination of energy and story. When we experience a strong emotion, we create a story that wraps around the feeling. Our story is important to our ego. We each have a favorite story that explains how we navigate through life.

❖ In order to access the inherent wisdom that resides in your knowing heart, I invite you to feel the impact of an emotion such as anger, blame, shame, despair, and guilt.

• Take a few gentle breaths and recall a time when you were angry or in pain. The first step is to remember to breathe into your high heart and invite yourself to be curious about someone who triggers a strong emotional reaction in you. Curiosity limits judgment and denial.

• Next, arouse your will and courage to dialogue with the feeling. Welcome your strong emotion. For example, "Hi, Anger, welcome. I see you have shown up in my life once again."

• The next crucial step is to interrupt the reactive pattern as it is happening. Be creative and try something different. For example, laugh out loud at yourself, take a walk, repeat the word "intention," or pat yourself on your high heart for being willing to break your trance. When you interrupt the pattern, new possibilities arise and your whole brain chemistry changes.

• Next, intentionally drop your story. It takes courage to interrupt your story. When you let go of your story, which serves as your emotional hot button, even for a couple of minutes, the emotions and the story line begin to dissolve.

• Reflect on how you link emotion and meaning by telling your story to explain, justify, or gain support for your emotions.

Moving Through Victim Consciousness

The measure of emotional health is the capacity to act with good will. Yet we all carry an inner blame that is transmitted from generation to generation. Victim consciousness is fear-based consciousness. The voice of victim consciousness announces, "My experience is always someone else's fault." Victim beliefs come from a deep sense of self-doubt about our self worth. Additional examples of self-doubt, which lead to self-judgment and victim consciousness, include:

- I will never be enough.
- I can never do enough.
- I do not have enough.
- I do not know enough.

What we project about who we are becomes how the world sees us. If we feel like a victim, others will treat us like a victim. In truth, in our unique ways we each cling to our limitations. Fear of transcendence is the major way our ego restricts access to our authentic self. In order to release ourselves from negative self-talk, we must take action. Only by taking action can we re-wire our brain for empowerment.

- ❖ Try this:
    - For one day, banish complaining and blaming and all of your favorite forms of negative thinking.
    - Switch your thinking from complaining to asking yourself, "What do I want to create instead of this?"
    - Next, reflect on the specific events and the meanings you attached to each event.
    - Take a breath and release your negative attachments to the past.
    - Finally, remember that love is forgiving, and the one who has the power is the one who forgives first. Extend amnesty to yourself and anyone else who deserves your love.
    - Now decide which friends you wish to accompany you into your future.
    - Take action.

The action does not need to be heroic. Reversing our identification with our ego can be as simple as treating ourselves with love instead of self-judgment. Convincing ourselves that we are inadequate or undeserving sets us up for shame and guilt. Melissa Eldridge spoke from her heart when she said in an interview, "Our biggest wounding is often our greatest gift to give." Make your wounds your teacher, and they will offer up their gifts.

Self-respect and a feeling of self worth attract a higher energy. According to Sasha Xarrian, author of *Outrageous Mastery,* feeling worthy leads to self-confidence. Self-confidence comes from loving who you are. If you wish to boost your self-confidence, move outside your comfort zone and reclaim your emotions. Your comfort zone and your self-confidence will expand each time you risk. You will experience more self-confidence each time you express your feelings. Emotional integrity promotes authenticity. Feeling worthy includes variations on the following beliefs:

- I deserve the best.
- I honor all of myself, and I expect others to honor me too.
- I am free to love myself and others with my whole soul.

Marianne Williamson offers a different perspective on fear. "Our greatest fear is not that we are inadequate; our deepest fear is that we are powerful beyond measure." What if we imagined that our power is the power of love, the power to create, the power to transform ourselves, our communities, our nations, and our planet?

The Power of Projections

Projections happen all the time, and they get in the way of authentic connections."
Kathlyn Kingdon, channeling for Djwhal Khul

Have you heard the old Irish saying about all of us living in each other's shadows? Reverend Lauren Artress, author of *Walking a Sacred Path: Rediscovering the Labyrinth as a Spiritual Tool,* points out, "If we're not aware of our anger, our jealousy, our fear, our hurt feelings, we project them outside ourselves onto others. The unkind things we do—the backbiting, the bigotry—occur simply because we don't know ourselves deeply enough to understand that whatever we criticize in another is also within." Shadow work is not intellectual; it's a journey from the head to the heart. Befriending and integrating your shadow will empower you to love more deeply and freely. Personal shadow includes rage, jealousy, shame, lying, resentment, lust, greed, suicidal and murderous tendencies, and addictions.

Since our shadow aspects are rooted in deep, unconscious patterns that control our behavior more than our conscious mind does, they limit our ability to make conscious choices. Shadow development runs parallel to ego development. Most of us are driven by the four-year-old child within us who didn't get our needs met. What doesn't fit our developing ego ideal—our idealized sense of self, individually reinforced by family and culture—becomes shadow. Our shadow shows us where we are incomplete. Feeling stuck is a signal that our shadow is in control.

We disown parts of ourselves because of our core beliefs, which are always tied to our family and early childhood. The debilitating judgments that are rooted in our shadow include:

- You're not okay.
- You're not lovable.
- You do not deserve.
- You are not worthy.

When we deny certain aspects of ourselves, we overcompensate by embracing their opposites. In other words, what you don't own, owns you. For example, leaders may project their inadequacies, healers may project their anger, and parents may project their fears.

Your commitment to your spiritual path will not shelter you from doing your personal shadow work. As Dr. Carl Jung said, "One does not become enlightened by imagining figures of light, but by making the darkness conscious."

To free ourselves from repressing or projecting our emotions, we need to acknowledge the feelings we have judged as negative. Anger, fear, and pain are not negative. When we deny or project any emotion, we compromise our ability to love. I challenge you to banish emotional censorship! Listen to the wisdom of Alan Watts, who wrote, "In order to be truthful you must embrace your whole being. A person who exhibits both positive and negative qualities, strengths and weaknesses, is not flawed but is complete. Because human consciousness must evolve both pleasure and pain, to strive for pleasure to the exclusion of pain, in effect, is to strive for loss of consciousness."

To the degree that you deny or reject an aspect of yourself, you will continually attract people into your life that will act out that aspect. The attraction or repulsion toward another person on whom we project our rejected emotions will be strong. Reflect on what you have given up to belong, to be loved, to be successful, or to be committed to your spiritual path.

Here's a useful shadow test proposed by Ken Wilber, author of *A Brief History of Everything*. If a person informs you, you are not projecting. However, if a person affects you, consider that a red flag which indicates the presence of your personal shadow. Another simple strategy to discover the nature of your own shadow is to ask yourself what sort of person you find most despicable or impossible to relate to. Welcome to your own shadow. Part of the core curriculum in this School of Love is to befriend and integrate your own shadow.

The most common way to deny a troublesome emotion is to paste the qualities you have rejected onto another person. I fell in love with an artist and projected my unclaimed creativity onto him. After we were married, he never picked up a paintbrush again. When I first recognized him as a shadow teacher for me, I vowed to cultivate my own creative self-expression. More recently, I projected my disowned anger onto a lover. I convinced myself that he possessed more than enough anger for both of us. Eventually, I experienced and expressed the power of my own anger. Then I left the relationship. He, too, became a shadow teacher for me.

Strategies for Shadow Integration

Gandhi said, "The only evils in the world are those running around in your heart. That is where the battle should be fought." Give the gifts of your heart to the shadow. As soon as you open your heart to yourself, you will open to others.

When I studied psychosynthesis, I learned about my shadow aspects through work with sub-personalities. Sub-personalities reveal behaviors that we find unacceptable within ourselves. Each sub-personality has a style and motivation of its own as well as a gift. My own shadow parade included Rowdy Rosie, Rosie the Wrestler, Rosie the Outsider, and Rosie the Wanderer. The challenging part of identifying and befriending each of my characters was to acknowledge their gifts. For example, Rowdy Rosie overflowed with energy, spontaneity, and play. Rosie the Wrestler was strong, persistent, focused and determined to win. Rosie the Outsider brought detachment as a gift. Finally, Rosie the Wanderer offered me a sense of independence, adventure, and freedom. Clearly, it was my judgment and denial of the above aspects of myself that blocked their gifts.

Dialoguing with each sub-personality is an entertaining way to uncover beliefs as well as motivations. For example, addressing Rowdy Rosie, I asked, "Will you allow me to speak to the part of you who enjoys being center stage and making a scene?" Once you create a dialogue, you can inquire about what your character needs, what its motivations are, as well as what gifts it brings. Once sub-personalities are embraced, they become resources for expanding our consciousness.

Noble Friends as Teachers

Has anyone ever told you about the role of a noble friend in your life? Noble friends are people you are destined to meet. Their job is to confront you with your own shadow as well as your light shadow, which includes your competencies and authenticity.

I do not enjoy the detailed work of editing. I do enjoy gathering lots of ideas, examples, research, and creating a gestalt or mandala. However, organizing and proofreading bores and frustrates me. A few times while editing this book, a persistent voice in my head challenged me to abort this project, demanding, "Who do you think you are to write this book?" My noble friend, Nancy Carlson, lovingly pointed out to me that paying attention to details is my shadow function. She was right!

Embracing Our Light Shadow

Remember that each of us also has a light shadow—our buried competence and authenticity. Once we reclaim our positive projections, we experience more freedom, peace, and joy. To identify your light shadow, think of a person you admire. Next, identify the specific qualities that you appreciate. Chances are that what you admire in another is your unacknowledged and unclaimed light shadow. I admire singers. Music often moves me to tears. Yet I was the only person in my high school who was rejected from joining the glee club. My singing voice became my light shadow and remained one until I forced myself to take singing lessons when I was 40 years old. Although you will probably never listen to a CD by me, I do love chanting in groups and leading singing in my workshops. Claiming my singing voice empowered me, even though it was more than two decades after the humiliation of being rejected by the director of the glee club. How about making a commitment right now to claim your own power?

❖ Here's a useful strategy to use when you wish to grow beyond your projection.

- Identify each person in your life for whom you hold judgment, blame, jealousy or adulation.
- Now adopt an attitude of friendly curiosity and imagine this person is giving you an opportunity to grow.
- Breathe into your high heart. Continue to breathe in love and breathe out love.
- Surround your teacher with love.
- Gently remember all the ways this person impacts you and surround each of the qualities that you have judged with love.
- Remind yourself once again that you nominated this person to be your designated teacher, and all is in divine order.

Switching Our Focus

Understanding that we have a choice in how we respond to and interpret our experiences brings healing to the emotional body. "Everything happens for you, not to you," Byron Katie, author of *Loving What Is,* insists. Instead of telling your story from start to finish, consider telling your story about what happened to you beginning in the middle. For example, I damaged my right kneecap a few years ago and a few weeks later ripped the tendons and ligaments in the same knee. I was in deep pain whenever I walked. I punished myself with many statements filled with self-blame and self-judgments: "How could you have injured yourself twice? What is wrong with you?" Eventually, I grew bored with my critical attitude and inquired about why the injury had happened for me. Beginning the story in the middle I wrote: "My painful knee injury happened for me. Sigh." Then I admitted to myself that I felt overloaded with too many responsibilities. I decided to meditate and concentrate on healing my attitudes and my knees. I also took more time to reflect and relax. As a bonus, I reconnected with a chiropractor, Dr. Malcolm Williams, whom I had not seen for twenty-five years. Together we collaborated on healing my injured knee without surgery.

Being aware of what we are feeling and giving ourselves permission to express our emotions empowers us to be more present for love and life.

Emotions also affect our consciousness and our behavior. Read on to discover how our emotions influence our awareness and our consciousness.

Reflective Emotion Questions

- Do you place your faith in your fears or in the Divine?
- What causes your heart to harden?
- What is your deepest wound—the one you hold on to and refuse to let go?
- Where in your life do you continue to suffer?
- What emotional, physical, mental, or spiritual wounds continue to dampen your love of self?

Awakening Reflection Responses

I invite you to reflect on the Emotions chapter and record your insights for this day.

- ❖ I Learned_____
- ❖ I Relearned_____
- ❖ I Discovered_____
- ❖ I Rediscovered_____
- ❖ I Regret_____
- ❖ I Appreciate_____
- ❖ Right Now I Feel_____
- ❖ And I Will_____

Journaling Prompts:

Here are a few prompts to give you more to wrap your all-knowing heart around. Feel free to agree, disagree, make your own connections, or write your own quotations.

"Nothing shapes our journeys through life so much as the questions we ask." Sam Keen

"We don't see things as they are, we see things as we are." Anais Nin

"An education devoid of the ecstatic moment is the mere shadow of education." George Leonard

"Take me to the exquisite edge of courage and release me to become." Sue Monk Kidd

"The universe is conscious, self creating, ever renewing, and always evolving to increasing levels of complexity and creativity." Deepak Chopra

The Conscious Continuum: Moving from Trance to Transcendence

Consciousness

Chapter Three

The Consciousness Spiral

Your beliefs become your thoughts.
Your thoughts become your words.
Your words become your actions.
Your actions become your habits.
Your habits become your values.
Your values become your destiny.
- Mahatma Gandhi

Awareness as Teacher

A group of Western spiritual leaders and teachers met in Santa Fe, New Mexico, in 2010, to discuss the current themes in consciousness. Each leader was interviewed separately afterwards, and a majority of the participants said they believed a significant shift in consciousness had happened since their meeting the prior year. Manifestation seemed to be losing momentum, and empowerment was the chosen frontrunner.

Our empowerment begins with awareness. Centuries ago, the Buddha taught that living in awareness was connected to living in the present moment. Moment to moment awareness reminds us that what worked yesterday may not serve us in the present moment. Why? The present moment is the only place of power. The focus of our awareness becomes our reality. We need to practice being aware in order to collect observations, thoughts, emotions and body sensations. Dr. Frances E. Vaughan writes, "Self-awareness is the foundation of psychological health and wellbeing."

Awareness opens our minds and hearts to new possibilities. Oriah Mountain Dreamer, author of *What We Ache for: Creativity and the*

Unfolding of the Soul, puts it this way: "Being aware is being willing to stay with what is and follow it without expectation, holding an attitude of genuine curiosity and open inquiry."

The first step to awareness is learning how to sense and then how to track the flow of energy into and out of our bodies. This requires conscious attention. You can grow your awareness by stopping whatever you are doing for at least two minutes several times a day to do an awareness check-in. Your ability to be effective is only as good as the accuracy of your perceptions. What we see and believe depends on the quality of our consciousness and the clarity of our awareness. Here's how to become more aware of your personal energy patterns:

❖ Dedicate a place in your journal to record your personal energy audit. Remember to date each entry.
- Stop whatever you are doing for at least two minutes.
- Focus on your breath. Gently inhale and exhale.
- Notice what you are aware of at this moment.
- Note what you are feeling.
- Rank your energy level using a scale of 1-10, with 1 being depressed, and 10 being elated.
- Take action.

Commit to making one change to increase your energy. For example, see what happens if you avoid negative conversations or gossiping. You might treat yourself to three minutes of residing in your high heart and remembering happy times—even if you have to escape to the bathroom for privacy. Another strategy is to write a short love note to yourself and put it somewhere where you will find it before the end of the day.

I challenge you to do this exercise at least twice a day for one month. I promise you that you will discover patterns and connections that add to your sense of aliveness.

Awareness as Empowerment

The conscious practice of awareness is staying with what is. To be aware is to be awake. We empower ourselves when we consciously focus our awareness on our thoughts, beliefs, and feelings.

❖ Here is another strategy to fine-tune your awareness. Remember to date your entry when you write in your journal.

- Set a timer for fifteen minutes. Record every thought, impression, and feeling that passes through your mind.
- At the end of fifteen minutes, read your list out loud and record your feelings. Then draw a heart around thoughts that energize and empower you.
- Next draw a line through thoughts that limit you or rob you of energy.
- Open your all-knowing heart to detect deeper patterns.
- Finish this exercise by writing, and now I will. _____
  _____.

Taking action is crucial to the awakening process. By accepting responsibility for making a change in your life, you are reprogramming your unconscious and expanding your self-confidence. To deepen this practice, record the time and your responses in a journal. Then you can track your growing awareness over days, weeks, and even months.

What we pay attention to determines how we feel moment by moment. I invite you to commit to monitoring and growing your energy and consciousness during the upcoming days, weeks, and months. Anne Lamott, author of *Grace Eventually*, promises, "There is ecstasy in paying attention. You can get into a kind of Wordsworthian openness to the world, where you see in everything the essence of holiness, a sign that God is implicit in all of creation." Remember that we all transmit our state of consciousness to everyone around us.

- ❖ Get ready to bring even more awareness to your consciousness by reflecting and then journaling:
  - Take a breath, change your physical posture, and identify where, when, and with whom you sense your energy leaks out or diminishes.
  - Identify where, when, and with whom you sense your energy flowing and alive.
  - Record what you noticed. How was your energy different? How can you make use of your observations?
  - And now I will_____.

Remember that you are the guardian of your consciousness. Taking action on your reflections creates deeper connections and meaning. Every breath you take, every decision you make, and every action you take aligns you with your sense of empowerment or victimhood. Like consciousness itself, there are levels of awareness that we can tap into and deepen:

- Ordinary awareness: everyday awareness.
- Witness awareness: not attached to anything or anyone. Its purpose is to bring us into unconditional presence so that we not only believe, but also know there is no physical or emotional state that has the power to knock us out of alignment.
- Spiritual awareness: perception through an intuitive grasp of the whole.
- Multidimensional awareness: familiarity with the many dimensions that coexist with our ordinary consciousness: fairies, spiritual guides, angels, inner earth beings, past and future lifetimes.

The Range of Consciousness

Think of consciousness as awareness that includes attention, intention, and memory. Remember that much of what we perceive as natural human behavior is actually the consequence of developmental programming. We can reprogram our lives by acquiring and acting upon new awareness.

Definitions of consciousness are as multifaceted as consciousness itself:

"Consciousness is the capacity to react to, attend to, and be aware of self and other."
- Francesca McCartney, author of *Body of Health*

"Consciousness is the field out of which everything is evolving."
- Barbara Marx Hubbard, author of *Emergence.*

"Consciousness is an infusing presence throughout the universe that enables us in cooperation with the brain, to connect meaningfully with the world beyond our physical body."
- Duane Elgin, author of *The Living Universe.*

"Human consciousness is somehow analogous to the holographic plate, and each of us actually contains the total information of all consciousness: past, present, and future."
- Dr. Brugh Joy, author of *Joy's Way.*

❖ Let's explore how you define consciousness:
   • Open your journal and write down the date.
   • Breathe into your all-knowing heart and tap into your wisdom.
   • Write your definition of consciousness. Feel free to borrow and combine ideas from the people cited above.
   • Save some space to revise or expand it as you grow your consciousness.

Our state of consciousness determines how we see the world. States of consciousness range from ordinary states, altered states, stoned states, and meditative states, to hypnotic states and cosmic states. Each aspect of consciousness has its own frequency. Our truth depends on where we are at any moment on the consciousness continuum. The lower frequencies constrict our energy and limit our perceptions, emotions, beliefs and possibilities. The higher frequencies of consciousness expand and transform our awareness, perceptions, feelings, choices, beliefs and purpose. We can change both our inner and outer worlds by changing our consciousness, and the choice is always ours.

The Nature of Conscious and Subconscious Minds

We must understand the nature of the mind and how the conscious and subconscious mind control our perceptions, beliefs, actions, and future. The more conscious we are of our thought process, the greater power we have to transform ourselves from the inside out. According to Marianne Williamson, author of *A Return to Love,* "Because thought is the creative level of things, changing our minds is the ultimate personal empowerment."

The conscious and subconscious minds are interdependent. The conscious mind is creative. It conjures up positive thoughts and creates intention. Explicit memories are clear, conscious recollections of specific events. The subconscious is responsible for the rest. Furthermore, the conscious mind is the place of free will and reminds us that we are not just victims of our programming. Conscious mind, the place of explicit beliefs, is responsible for imagining, deciding, and taking short-term action. Yet according to research, it is only responsible for about 2% of thoughts, feelings, and behaviors.

In contrast, the subconscious mind is strictly habitual; it will play the same behavioral responses to life's signals over and over again. According to Dr. Bruce Lipton, author of *Matter and Miracles*, "When it comes to sheer neurological processing abilities, the subconscious mind is millions of times more powerful than the conscious mind."

The subconscious mind keeps a meticulous record of everything you have ever experienced during your lifetime. It records how you felt and what you believed about each event. Instead of forming perceptions based on the sensations and awareness of the moment, the subconscious mind cross-references the incoming perceptions with experiences from your past.

The subconscious mind, the place of implicit memories, is responsible for all the other 98% of our perceptions, emotions, and behaviors. Implicit memories are residue traces of past experiences that exist outside of awareness and powerfully shape our lives. Implicit beliefs are grounded in doubts, anxieties, and sabotaging behaviors. Anything that is impressed on the subconscious mind becomes hard-wired by repetitive action.

If you wish to expand your consciousness and move beyond your limited ego, the place to begin is with unconscious, implicit memories. In order to experience long-term results, we need to reprogram our subconscious mind. Think of how many times you made a New Year's resolution and stuck to your promise for a few days, only to fall back into old behavior. Chances are you had an unconscious implicit belief that interfered with your best intentions. In order to experience long-term results, we need to reprogram our subconscious mind. If you want to expand your consciousness and move beyond your limited ego, begin with your unconscious, implicit memories.

The good news is that your subconscious mind cannot tell the difference between reality and an imagined thought or image. That is one of the reasons for the success of visualization and imagery techniques. If you act *as if* you believe a new thought, you can successfully bypass the restrictive aspect of your unconscious. The world mirrors yourself back to you. If you love, nourish, and appreciate yourself internally, it will show up in your external life. Dr. Bruce Lipton reminds us that consciousness, which includes our beliefs about what is real and possible, has as much as 100 times more power to affect our well-being than any material force including drugs and surgery.

Dr. Candace Pert, author of *Molecules of Emotion*, writes, "The more conscious we are, the more we can listen in on the conversations going on at an autonomic or subconscious level of our mind/body. Only then can we enter into that conversation, using our awareness to enhance the effectiveness of the autonomic system where health and disease are being determined minute to minute."

The Changing Nature of Consciousness

Change is a result of a shift in consciousness. When you open yourself up to believe that there are no limitations to human consciousness, you are treated to a flow of information and guidance. Awakened consciousness is a state of being aware that you are aware. It is the realization that you are the watcher, the witness within you—not the analyst, not the thinker, not even the meditator, but that which is the impartial witness of every aspect of your being and doing."

Each of us creates a vibrational field of consciousness that mirrors our current mental, emotional, and spiritual state. Robert Monroe, author of *Ultimate Journey,* writes, "The spectrum of consciousness ranges, seemingly endlessly, beyond time-space into other energy systems. It also continues downward through animal and plant life, possibly into the sub-atomic level. Everyday human consciousness is active commonly in only a small segment of the consciousness continuum." Once we entertain the idea that we are primarily spiritual beings working through the limitations of physical bodies, our consciousness begins to expand. According to Seth, a disembodied spiritual teacher who channeled through Jane Roberts, author of *Seth Speaks*: "Throughout your vibrational existences, you expand your consciousness, your ideas, your perceptions, your values. You break away from self-adopted restrictions, and you grow spiritually as you learn to step aside from limiting conceptions and dogma."

I know from my own experience that as our consciousness changes and expands, our soul purpose also transforms. In addition, our guides and teachers may also change. Each year I conduct a review of my guides and teachers to make sure that all are still in alignment with my present soul purpose. Occasionally, I find a few who are ready to serve others. I honor their commitment and thank each one for their love and perspective. The passing of guides feels like a graduation, and I always feel filled with gratitude rather than grief. Then, suddenly my very familiar and long present guides disappear and I open up my high heart and welcome new guides.

The only exception happened when my third eye chakra popped open in April 2010. Suddenly, I inherited a new guide, but I grieved for my familiar spiritual friends and teachers. Actually, I stomped around the house until I admitted my ego was running my show. When I breathed and calmed down and inquired about the deeper truth, I realized I was upset about not having any warning or the opportunity to say "goodbye " and "Godspeed" to my guides. Then I intuited that a deeper pattern was affecting me, and I committed myself to staying with my inner unfolding process. Then I connected the sudden death of my teenaged son, Mike, to my grief and suffering for not being able to say "goodbye" to either Mike or my guides. Later that night I had a healing dream and felt more mature in the morning.

Consciousness is grounded in beliefs. Seldom do we take the time to think about and reflect on our personal and cultural beliefs. Yet the way we react and behave and relate to others is connected to our beliefs. That is why we require a class about beliefs in our School of Love.

Beliefs as Builders of Consciousness

Beliefs are something that you place value on and identify with. "Belief is the place where all true change originates," writes Margaret Wheatley, author of *Leadership and the New Science*. Everything is both referenced through our belief system and limited by it. Indeed, much of what we perceive as natural human behavior is actually the consequence of developmental programming that took place before we entered second grade

Quantum science reveals that our power to control our lives originates from our minds and is not preprogrammed in our genes. Imagine that your mind is like a computer that needs to be constantly programmed with updated information about your beliefs and intentions. Our beliefs reflect our state of consciousness.

Did anyone ever tell you that thought is an action? Every feeling we have is an action. Every word we speak is an action. Both quantum theory and contemporary research in human perception suggest that over 80% of what we see in the external world is a function of internal assumptions and beliefs. Most people don't realize that when they discard an old belief and/or adopt a new one, they have taken an action that modifies how they see and make meaning out of their world.

Your beliefs affect not only your reality but also your body. "Beliefs control biology," according to Dr. Bruce Lipton. Your physical body is a biofeedback system for your attitudes and beliefs. Perceptions and beliefs not only control behavior, they control gene behavior as well. Bruce Lipton puts it this way: "When someone has a sudden shift of belief, it can radically change your genetic code, the way your genes interpret life. This could be the difference between cancer and remission."

Beliefs are not facts. We are free to change our beliefs and their accompanying meaning. If we are wedded to a limiting belief, we have no room to expand our consciousness. When we banish a limited belief, we dissolve the emotional context and free our imaginations to create more empowering beliefs.

Gregg Braden, author of *The Divine Matrix,* reminds us: "From the healing of disease, to the length of our lives, to the success of our career and relationships, everything that we experience is directly related to what we believe." We are only as free as our beliefs allow us to be. Our beliefs hold all of the power we need for all of the change we choose.

In order to rid myself of negative thinking, I participated in a prosperity consciousness experiment at Unity Church. I wanted to become more aware of the ways I sabotaged myself, and friends had warned me that this was not an exercise for sissies. I set a specific goal and I committed myself to refrain from all forms of negative thinking for 28 days. Each time I expressed a negative idea or feeling, I had to begin on day one again. In addition, I wore a string bracelet that I switched from one wrist to the opposite wrist each time I interrupted my positive flow with a negative thought or emotion.

Twice I reached 16 days without a negative interruption, and both times I lost my positive focus while I was driving. My solution, after the second time this happened, was to refrain from driving for 12 days. Feeling self-satisfied and self-confident, and more than a little cocky, I looked forward to 12 more days of success.

On the third sixteenth day, my washing machine broke and I had an interview scheduled and needed to show up in clean clothes. I walked to the laundromat and loaded the washing machine—only to realize I had not brought detergent or quarters! I became a prisoner of my own negative thoughts. I was even more determined to harness my negative thinking. It took me four months to be free from negativity for 28 consecutive days. This experiment in consciousness pointed out to me how many times I added my personal negative thinking to the creation of a collective negative consciousness. I also realized that each time I had a negative thought about someone else, I was also hurting myself!

Negative self-talk creates negative moods. If you are being plagued by a negative thought, simply say out loud "next" or switch the negative thought into a positive, high frequency belief. When I am aware of a persistent negative thought, I take a deep breath and repeat to myself, "God is…" and continue adding my positive beliefs to the open statement until the negative thought dissolves, as it always does, because we cannot hold two contradictory thoughts at the same time.

Questioning and updating each of our beliefs to align with our soul purpose entrains us to experience more freedom, presence, and authenticity. I challenge you to update your beliefs and to align with self-love, joy, empowerment, creativity, healing, and celebration of life. Remember that every thing that happens in your life is both referenced through your belief system and limited by it.

❖ You can deepen your awareness about your personal beliefs by pondering these questions:
   • What belief is sustaining or undermining my action?
   • What do I gain by this belief?
   • Is this belief expansive or contractive?
   • What would I have to give up or do to change this belief?
   • What does my all-knowing heart yearn for in this moment?

Belief Creates Reality

According to Rick Hanson, co-author of *Buddha's Brain,* a revolution in neuroscience has recently revealed that the adult brain remains open to change throughout its lifetime. When we change our mind, our brain changes. In other words, the brain becomes what the mind does. Hanson reminds us that how we focus our attention, how we intentionally direct the flow of energy and information through our neural circuits can directly alter the brain's activity and its structure.

Whenever we experience something, we create neural network circuits in our brain. When we repeat the experience, we reinforce the neural networks. Then our brain causes us to think, feel, and to take action or not based on our beliefs. Becoming aware of what we fill our mind with is the first step toward growing our consciousness. Why? We become whatever we think. Our brain is 100% responsible for insuring that our external world matches the internal world of our implicit beliefs.

People are not moved, changed or challenged by circumstances; rather, people change and challenge circumstances by what they feel and think. Sovereignty begins and ends in the thought realm. Remember that our beliefs affect our behavior and our ability to create the life we desire and deserve. Mind/body responds as a unit. No thought, no emotion is without biochemical, electrochemical activity; and the activity leaves no cell untouched.

Our unconscious programming will rule our thinking, feeling and relating. What does this information mean for you personally? If you harbor a belief that you are unworthy, unlovable, or unsafe, your negative conviction will override even your strongest intention!

When I do soul readings, I have the opportunity to view the results of crucial turning points in a person's life, and I can identify the individual's strongest beliefs based on their decisions. For example, a woman who consulted me had a hard time acknowledging her competence. Even though she had received three promotions in one year, she dismissed herself as "lucky, I guess." When I confronted her with her shadowboxing statement and asked where this limiting belief originated she said, "My grandfather. He told me never to stand out or I would be doomed to failure, just like he was." She cried as she continued. "He taught me to be really, really careful."

"Is that belief true for you? Does it align with your soul's truth," I asked.

"Not entirely," she said in a little girl voice.

"What part is true?' I persisted.

"Well, actually none of it fits." She said, raising her head and her voice. Until she was able to affirm her competency without fear, her limiting beliefs would keep her hostage.

The universe always says "yes" to our strongest belief or fear. When we are not aware of our inner beliefs, we set ourselves up to become victims of them. In other words, our present reality is an accurate mirror of our strongest beliefs about ourselves, others, and the world. Tell me what you believe and I will tell you what your life experience looks like on the outside. Our personal beliefs either resonate with empowerment or victim hood.

❖ I adapted the following exercise from Michael Dowd, author of *Thank God for Evolution.*

- Choose a time when you felt like a victim or you victimized yourself. First, write about the incident from a victim's viewpoint. Feel free to exaggerate, be dramatic and fully engage this aspect of your consciousness. Take a breath and release the story.
- Next, write the same story from a victor's viewpoint. Feel free to exaggerate and be playful as well as powerful.
- Now take a breath and prepare to write the story as a practical joke that God orchestrated in order to remind you to take yourself lightly.

The Power of Limited Beliefs

We build our lives on the foundation of our stories. The more we believe our stories, the more we energize our beliefs. By remembering events that resonated with low energy, you re-enter the frequency of the event. Worrying, complaining, fearing, blaming, and judging vibrate with low energy. Drama, too, is a low energy attractor. When we talk about what we don't want or complain or blame, we are stuck in that low vibration, and we will attract low energy people and situations. For example, I consulted with a woman who had experienced an abusive relationship with a man. When she called she started to relate every detail of her experience. I told her I did not need to know the details. I was more interested in how her experience connected to her current beliefs as well as her soul's path. We scheduled a phone session. Before her scheduled telephone session, she e-mailed me a three-page history of the abusive relationship, which I deleted without reading a word.

When she called for her consultation, she reported she had barely survived a fierce migraine. I was not surprised. I pointed out to her that she had re-traumatized herself by writing all the details again. Before we completed the session, I advised her to practice the "Wipe and Flush" technique, remembering that before we flush our waste products down the toilet, we do not examine each piece, we simply wipe and flush.

A study at the National Science Foundation reported that deep thinkers think around 50,000 thoughts a day. This study also cited that 95% of what most people think is negative. Furthermore, they concluded that 90% of what people think one day is carried over to the next. Negative thinking is an addiction and drains energy. Instead of asking, "Why does this happen *to* me?" engage in a deeper consciousness than the one that created the problem. Dare to shift your awareness and inquire, "Why does this happen *for* me?" You are the only one in charge of your consciousness. In order to shift your consciousness from victim or martyr to victor, Sasha Xarrian, author of *Outrageous Mastery*, suggests the following activities:

❖ Write a list of 50 lessons or gifts you gained from so-called failure.

❖ Write another list of anything positive that anyone has ever said about your life.

❖ Make a commitment to honor yourself for the person you have been today.

The Principle of Attraction

The universal law of attraction works like this: you attract whatever you focus on. Low expectation is connected to limiting beliefs. The shorthand explanation is positive picture/positive action/positive outcome. Tracking our beliefs is an important step toward expanding our consciousness and aligning with our authentic self. The belief that you are a victim results in misery and drama. Anytime you convince yourself that someone did something bad or evil to you, you are energizing a victim consciousness. Believing you are a victim keeps you in a suffering cycle of feeling powerless. In order to experience an authentic life, we must choose to replace our victim beliefs with empowering beliefs. Without making an internal shift in consciousness and choosing an empowering set of beliefs, we recreate the old, dysfunctional patterns in our lives, regardless of new opportunities.

According to Dr. Leonard Laskow, "The beliefs we hold within us tend to become self-fulfilling prophecies. We find in the external world experiences that support our inner beliefs. Simply put, we see what we once believed we saw, not what is." The limiting beliefs that you are not safe or valued or loved, or that your needs and feelings are too much compared to others are low frequency error thoughts that move you in the direction of believing you are a victim. Reverend August Gold, author of *Thank You God for Everything,* emphasizes, "The human part of our consciousness is entrenched in victim consciousness." When you are entangled in victim consciousness, it is difficult to embrace the understanding of how you create your own misery. Unreleased negative thought results in a negative condition. Here are some examples of negative personal beliefs or default scripts:

• I am unworthy.

- My feelings, thoughts, and needs do not matter.
- I am powerless.
- Happiness does not last.
- Relationships only cause pain.
- My life does not matter.

Continuing to uproot implicit beliefs in your unconscious is an act of courage. We can change only that which we are conscious of experiencing.

❖ In order to move closer to your authentic self, I invite you to return to your journal and record your truth as you ponder the following questions
  - In what areas of your life do you feel you have been or continue to respond as a victim? Write down as many as you can think of.
  - What are the gifts involved in those challenges? Take a gentle breath, change your posture, and write down what comes to you.
  - What have you learned about yourself?

After I did this exercise, I wrote a letter to a person to whom I had previously given my power away, thus abandoning myself:

Thank you for not listening to my feelings. I learned to listen to my own needs and feelings and to take action.

Thank you for lying to me. I learned to trust my intuition and discern between what I wanted to hear and what was real.

Thank you for criticizing me. I learned to recognize my own personal shadow and eventually accept myself more deeply.

When I finished writing the letter, I no longer felt judgmental or sorry for myself. Instead, I experienced healing and a sense of freedom. I put the letter in an envelope, addressed it, and put it in the mailbox. I did not receive a thank you note in return.

I do not know if the following ritual is factual or mythological. I never participated in a Native American women's circle, but the story I heard more than once goes like this. Any Native American woman is welcome to the talking circle. Everyone has an opportunity to speak when the talking stick reaches her hands. Newcomers are invited to tell their stories without interruptions or feedback. If invited, women in the circle share their experiences without telling the speaker what to do. If the woman returns to the circle with the same problem a second time, every woman listens respectfully and can offer their "heart wisdom" if invited. However, if the newcomer approaches the circle of women the third time with the same story and no subsequent action or change, the entire circle turns their backs on the woman.

When I first heard about this ritual, I experienced two opposite feelings. My first reaction was judgment. "How could a group of women reject one of their own who was in crisis?" My next reaction was, "How perfect. Since she did not listen to the accumulated experience of the other women, why allow her to eat up the energy and attention of the group?" You see, I was raised to believe that if I listened compassionately, my friend would eventually hear the voice of her own soul. However, if my friend identified herself as a victim, more often she would agree with my advice and then reject my idea and herself by saying, "Yes, but…" I developed "compassion fatigue" until I realized that turning my back and ignoring the repetitive story was an act of empowerment for both of us. I had to update my belief about listening, supporting, healing, and friendship before I could turn my back without feeling like a victim myself. Turning around our thinking is an empowering act and aligns us with our authentic self.

According to Dr. Martin Seligman, "The most convincing way to release a negative belief is to show it is factually incorrect."

❖ Here is an exercise to help you identify victim beliefs.
- Think about a challenge in your life that you perceived as having negative consequences.
- Ask yourself, what is my evidence for this belief? Notice what happens to your energy when you challenge your negative beliefs by providing facts.
- What beliefs were challenged?
- How did you react?
- Next, fast-forward yourself ahead a few years. What were the lessons?
- What beliefs did you sacrifice? What new beliefs did you plant in your consciousness as result of the lesson?

Inherited Beliefs

One of the goals of inner work is to become aware of our inherited family beliefs, our emotional blockages, and our personal limiting beliefs.

The beliefs you were raised with reside in your cells. According to Miguel Ruiz, "Whenever we hear an opinion and believe it, we make an agreement and it becomes part of our belief system." Remember that you adopted your primary beliefs from parents or other authority figures. When we consider that we inherited most of our family beliefs—including cultural and intergenerational beliefs—before we entered second grade, completing a belief inventory seems wise. Why? Our adopted family beliefs, especially the unconscious ones, may not support our spiritual journey and desire to live an authentic life.

In order to identify implicit beliefs, start by being honest about your life. When you identify an aspect of your life that does not measure up to your potential and dreams, begin your treasure hunt for deeply-rooted implicit beliefs. John Assaraf, author of *Having It All,* urges us to look at the results of our life if we wish to identify the implicit memories and the beliefs that generated the results.

❖ When you pay attention to your thoughts, what do you hear yourself saying about your relationship with each of the following?
  • Love
  • Relationships
  • Sexuality
  • Success
  • Power
  • Happiness
  • Health
  • Creativity
  • Dying and Death

After you have identified your core beliefs, the next step is altering your blueprint. Keep in mind that you are actually re-wiring your brain by creating new neural networks to support and achieve competence and freedom.

I focused on tracking my belief about success. Why? I am aware that when I reached a certain level, no matter what career path I pursued, I allowed myself only limited success. My implicit belief about success began as a loud voice in my head demanding, "Who do you think you are?" My limiting belief told me I could only be only a bit more successful than my friends. My controlling implicit belief centered on my fear of outshining my friends. My error belief centered around being abandoned if I became more successful than family or friends.

I was dumbfounded when I dug up the root cause of this and discovered that while I had been teaching others about women's fears about breaking rank, or stepping out of line by exceeding group expectations, I was doing exactly that. For example, in my family, success was reserved for men. My mother and her mother were homemakers. I was the first college graduate in my family. They passed down to me the belief that I would marry and be content raising children. In other words, men venture out into the world and enjoy success. Women stay at home and enjoy having babies and raising children. I bought it unconsciously, and it held me back until I uncovered the belief and released my learned limitations.

Reprogramming Your Brain

Affirmations work. However, if you hold a limiting implicit belief about success in your unconscious mind, the power of that negative belief will overwhelm your most passionate affirmation. Here's why. The principle of attraction dictates that our life mirrors our implicit beliefs. Our brain searches for people and events that match our implicit memories and beliefs. Reprogramming the implicit memories in your brain is the key to your long-term success.

<u>Step One</u>: Reset your implicit thermostat. For example, I set my internal success thermostat for 98.6 and made a logo of a thermostat and placed it in my house and car.

<u>Step Two</u>: Create an affirmation that includes what you desire to create as well as your doubts, anxieties, and past history. Since everything coexists, by including your shadow aspect you are creating a unified field. My affirmation was: I deserve to be outrageously successful beyond my imagination, even though I do not have a precise picture of what that looks like.

<u>Step Three</u>: Write down all your personal beliefs that support your new breakthrough belief. For example, I wrote: I have all the competencies, skills, and soul power I need to create and sustain outrageous success. I celebrate my easy and graceful success. I enjoy receiving the abundant support of my friends. I delight in using my success as a form of service to assist others who desire to expand beyond what they imagined possible.

Step Four: Consciously activate the beta, alpha, and delta brain frequencies of your mind to create coherence between implicit and explicit memories. Beta is the alert everyday state of consciousness that you use to create your affirmation. Next, move your consciousness to alpha, which is the quiet, relaxed meditative state of consciousness that resides within your subconscious mind. Finally, firm up your affirmation by accessing the delta brainwave frequency, the psychic soul force that connects you to universal consciousness. This is the dream state. Before you go to sleep, program your dreams to align with your new belief.

Step Five: Activate over-belief. This is full faith. Breathe in and feel the strength of your expansive, positive belief. Breathe in again and feel the power and passion of your belief so strongly that nothing stands between you and outrageous success. Remember that the subconscious mind does not discern between reality and imagination. Since implicit beliefs are stored as feelings and sensations, ground your success in your body by feeling what success feels, tastes, sounds, and smells like. Experience what you would feel when sharing your success story with friends, family, and God. Embody your belief by walking around the room, knowing that you are programming success into your brain and your cells! Exaggerate your physical expectation of success so it becomes an over-belief. Feel how you will feel in body, mind, and spirit as you walk as though it were already true.

Step Six: Savor the belief experience: Savoring is the deliberate conscious attention to the awareness of pleasure. According to Fred B. Bryant and Joseph Veroff, the four kinds of savoring are:

Basking: receiving praise and congratulations

Thanksgiving: expressing gratitude and blessings

Marveling: losing the self in the wonder of the moment

Luxuriating: indulging the senses

Focus on your emotions and body sensations, since they are the essence of implicit memory. Savoring boosts the immune system, aids concentration, and helps to steady the mind, because it releases dopamine. Imagine celebrating your breakthrough. Imagine soaking every cell with the juice of your success. Stay with your positive feelings. The longer you can hold a positive experience in your awareness, the more emotionally stimulating it becomes, and the more neurons fire and wire together to create a stronger trace memory. By focusing on the rewarding aspects of your experience, you increase the continuing release of dopamine, which strengthens neural associations in your implicit memory.

Step Seven: Extend gratitude. Send out your thanks in advance for achieving your goal. The frequency of gratitude is high and attracts other high-frequency emotions and events. Remember your subconscious does not know the difference between reality and fantasy. That is the reason why acting "as if" works!

Step Eight: Take one specific action each day for at least thirty days to align your brain with your intention. Research states that it takes from 30 to 90 days to change your habits and beliefs. That's why persistence is required if you want to achieve the changes you desire.

Step Nine: Give back. The principle of being in an attitude of gratitude invites you to give back as an example of reciprocity in action. Identify a person, place, or cause that has nurtured you. Donate time, energy, or money as a demonstration of your goal.

I am delighted to report that I now have friends who urge me to be outrageously successful. We have committed to being cheerleaders for each other's souls. Together and individually we break through layers of our own limitations. We celebrate each other and honor our heroics. Occasionally, I will embarrass myself and regress to old ways, but never for long.

Here's a recent e-mail from my long time friend Alison Strickland that I received after bragging about a recent breakthrough: "When Rosie's on her game, the universe responds abundantly." And here is a response from another dear friend from far away in Hawaii but close to my soul. Dr Julianne Hanson e-mailed me after I had taken a creative risk that felt scary: "Darling! You're apologizing to me for being fabulous? I don't think so. Don't know what you are used to in the female friendship realm, but I am indeed one of those women who celebrate my sisters' achievements—your accomplishments are my victories."

It is possible to break rank with our own self-imposed limitations, and joy, ease, and grace are the bonuses. If we can reprogram our thoughts, feelings, and consciousness, we can also reprogram our own personal blueprint to attain any goal we desire.

The Power of Joyful Beliefs

Miguel Ruiz, author of *The Four Agreements,* reminds us, "It is of supreme importance that you recognize the existence of joyful beliefs. If you want to live a life of joy and fulfillment, you have to find the courage to break those agreements that are fear-based and claim your personal power."

The principles of quantum physics suggest that by redirecting our attention and activating our will, we can create beliefs that support the values of our knowing hearts. Identify your negative, limiting beliefs, and you will find that updating your positive beliefs to reflect your soul's potential will affect everything in your life. You will grow in self-confidence and personal empowerment as well as reinforce your mastery in relation to the future.

You are at a choice point every moment of your life. A positive belief attracts high energy, which strengthens and empowers you. The energies of love, harmony, healing, trust, and forgiveness vibrate at a high frequency. The simple act of remembering times when you felt loving, trusting, and forgiving automatically raises your energy and empowers you to attract even more energy of a stronger frequency. On the other hand, a limiting belief attracts a low energy, which weakens you. If you identify a limiting belief such as "life is always difficult," be alert. The words "always" and "never" signal an emerging limited belief. Remember when Yoda reminded Luke Sky Walker of his limiting beliefs in Star Wars: "Weapons will do you no good in that cave, Luke. You will find only what you bring in with you."

Beliefs and intention support one another, just like intention and manifestation support each other. One action leads to the next action. Since we are the only guardians of our consciousness, we must learn how to master our intentions in this School of Love if we wish to become adapt at manifestation. Prepare yourself to claim your right to create the future you dream. The claiming and manifesting process is simply an extension of your consciousness.

Multidimensional Consciousness

The full potential of the multidimensional human mind is to tap into all of the knowledge through time, including the future. By intentionally expanding our consciousness, we gain the ability to experience the profound patterns of the universe. I believe that Emily Dickinson, a reclusive New England poet of the mid 1880's, understood the potential of living in multidimensional consciousness when she wrote, "I dwell in possibilities."

Quantum Thinking

As we adopt an expanded way of thinking, feeling, and being, our tendencies to reduce our world to either/or, good/bad, friend/adversary, which are hallmarks of linear thinking, fall away. Pepper Lewis, author of *Gaia Speaks*, writes, "Duality is something that people emerge from as they arrive at the center or heart of their life or perhaps a reality that has become obsolete." Other examples of polarities include: trust/doubt, soul/ego, clarity/confusion, forgiveness/withholding, grace/disgrace, and abundance/ scarcity.

This entry from my journal emphasizes how linear thinking limits our understanding and even our experience:

Out of the blue, I felt an overwhelming need to travel to Bali. I needed to remember something important about sacred dance. I knew nothing more.

During my first lesson, I felt awkward and frustrated trying to coordinate my hands, arms, eyes, and feet. Both the unfamiliar rhythm and the music hurt my ears! I tried too hard to memorize the intricate movements, and my body felt rigid and sore.

"What's wrong with me?" I asked myself countless times. "What am I blocking? Why is this so hard if I knew how to do it in a past lifetime? Or is my intuition about needing to travel halfway around the world to reclaim something a delusion?"

I labored and complained for two weeks while I struggled to memorize the movements. Several times, our skillful dance teacher ordered me to lie on the floor and practice the movements with my hands and let my feet enjoy a break. That made me feel even more hopeless. Laughter and delight eluded me.

After 14 days of consecutive practice for four hours a day (56 grueling hours), I decided to give myself a break. I heard loud gamelan music in the distance. Like someone under a spell, I ran in the direction of the familiar music. My heart quickened. My body vibrated. I recognized the rhythm of music and it felt like each cell in my body was exploding with recognition! I ran to the small bamboo house on the edge of the greening rice fields. My feet felt like they were on fire.

I knocked on the door of the house of music. I had not planned what I would say. A tall, muscular man dressed in a traditional white sarong opened the door. He smiled as I stammered that I remembered the music.

I saw four young men warming up for the dance. As I nodded to each of them, I began to remember the steps to the sacred Clown Dance. Instinctively I knew that this was the dance that magnetized me to fly to Bali. Furthermore, I knew intuitively that as I retraced the steps of the dance I would remember even more. Time was running out. I only had one more week in Bali.

The man at the door, Marti G. Mart, was the chief choreographer of sacred men's dance for the island of Bali! What are the odds of running into him on an unscheduled walk through the rice paddies? He looked straight into my eyes and said, "But, lady, you don't understand. The Clown Dance is a sacred dance. Only for men. Women are not allowed to see it. Ever."

I took one step backwards. Then I regained my balance and voice and stammered, "No, you don't understand. I know the steps. I even remember how the steps go together. Please let me show you. I have traveled all the way here from New Mexico, in the United States, to remember this dance." He shook his head from side to side and I feared that his gesture meant "no." Without one more word, I rushed past him to the dance floor, and began to move to the music. My eyes, shoulders and hands remembered how to move in unison. As I continued to move to the music, I felt harmony erupt from deep inside of me. I giggled. At last I felt like I was "flirting with the gods" as Son-ai-yu had tried to teach how me to do. Minutes passed, and when the music ended, I crumpled to the floor in a mixture of exhilaration and exhaustion.

Marti G. Mart hunched down next to me and hugged me. The four young men approached cautiously and surprised me with sounds of delight. Relief flooded me and I laughed from the bottom of my belly like a man!

For seven memorable days I studied with the men. Secretly. Marti G. Mart never said a word while we practiced. He demonstrated, and we imitated for six hours a day. My body filled in what I did not consciously remember. My intuition whispered guidance. I felt graced.

My guidance was correct. I needed to travel to Bali to reclaim sacred dance and reinvest in my body. I also needed to re-experience how ancient ritualistic movement created a sense of harmony, ecstasy, and peacefulness within my consciousness. The only obstacle was my misperceptions. The notion that I was a "male" dancer had never entered my consciousness.

Expanded thinking resonates with both/and. The fundamental shift is from knowing to discovering, from winning/losing to sharing, from doing/achieving to becoming and being." Deborah L. Johnson reminds us, "Duality is a place of deep separation. It is a place of contrast and comparison. It is a place of judgment." To the degree that we convince ourselves that we are certain of anything or anyone, we restrict our consciousness. Try Craig Hamilton's way of tapping into multidimensional consciousness by affirming, "I don't know and I want to know." This expansive practice tests your willingness to surrender to mystery and wonder. The unknown is the realm of possibility.

Noah and I had a conversation about the unknown one early morning when he wanted my attention while I sat in bed writing

<u>Noah</u>: "How many more pages do you have to write for your book?"
<u>Rosie</u>: "I don't know, Noah—a lot."
<u>Noah</u>: "You don't know because God has not told you yet, right Grandmom? I hope you only have to write three more pages so we can do pillow talk."

The new shift in consciousness is related to quantum thinking. By consciously choosing what is not known and being open to discovering what could manifest, we align with multidimensional consciousness.

We were taught that nothing travels faster than the speed of light. However, Russian physicists have discovered torsion waves that travel at the order of 10 to the 9th power—one billion times the speed of light!

Quantum thinking principles include the following:
- Expansion is continuous and circular like the spiral.
- All realities coexist in parallel dimensions and emit different frequencies.
- Expansion is the keynote. The movement is towards greater and greater wholeness.

According to quantum theory, in which all things coexist simultaneously, all probabilities must coexist for nature to be in harmony. If we apply this theory to our humanness, we would relate to ourselves as light and shadow, ego and essence, as well as multidimensional beings. I challenge us to open our minds and hearts and begin to consider the possibility of other invisible dimensions that coexist with what we regard as our "normal" reality.

One of the intriguing principles about quantum living is that there are no rules. Unlimited possibilities replace rules, and experience overrides knowledge. Imagine your body as an energetic laser antenna, receiving and sending energetic signals throughout all dimensions simultaneously. Now open your imagination to what might happen if you made an intention to remember or gain information about your multidimensional nature.

Open the possibility of your all-knowing mind to the essence of this dialogue between my guides and me:

Rosie: What is mind without words?

Guides: Energy. You are also capable of interacting and communicating directly with your multidimensional mind.

Rosie: What are the advantages?

Guides: There is no unconscious or shadow when you engage your multidimensional mind. Drama, politics, subterfuge become obsolete.

Rosie: It sounds more energy-efficient than the ways I've been brought up knowing.

Guides: Quantum knowing is directly related to your soul commitment. Yes, it is a commitment to override almost all the ways you have learned how to know.

Rosie: I have a hunch this way of "minding" is related to the research I have been doing on quantum thinking.

Guides: The essence of quantum thinking is the ability to access energy mind.

Rosie: In other words, you are referring to universal mind.

Guide: Remember all is energy. Thoughts are energy. Emotions are energy. Memories are energy. Energy announces itself in frequencies. Mind is a frequency transmitter and receiver. This is not an evolutionary development. It has always been so. Humans are now at an evolutionary precipice and are capable of embracing, exploring, and expanding into multidimensionality. The essence of that expansion calls upon each person to embrace self as an energy being who has inherited a quantum mind.

Rosie: Everyone is capable of knowing everything. I believe I have always known that possibility existed, but I lacked the knowledge of how to achieve and sustain that way of knowing and being.

Guides: Not any more.

David Spangler writes, "We live in more than one dimension at once. We are physical beings, but at the same time we are inhabitants of a spiritual reality that embraces and transcends the physical dimension."

❖ I invite you to tap into your wisdom dimension.
  - Take a few gentle breaths and breathing in and out your high heart. Open your journal and write: "Dearly Beloved, thank you for your guidance about my multidimensional nature." Let your words flow. Enjoy the experience. Remember you can create a dialogue or a soliloquy.
  - When you feel finished, send out your thanks.
  - Take a moment and reflect on what you have learned. What connections did you make? In what ways can you use this information to add to your presence?

Consider, for example, that for many people extrasensory experiences seem extraordinary because the only knowledge that counts as reality is knowledge that comes from their five physical senses. However, if you imagine yourself as both a cosmic being and a human being, you have access to knowledge and truths from many dimensions.

Several years ago I listened to Gregg Braden tell a story about a Native American medicine man from Taos Pueblo. He invited Gregg to witness him conducting a rain ritual. When Gregg asked the medicine man how he prayed for rain, he replied, "I pray rain. I remember how rain tastes and smells and how it feels on my head. I do not pray *for* rain." Out of myriad available choices, the wise medicine man chose the rain dimension because he knew from experience that it already coexisted with all of the other possibilities.

According to quantum physics, each observable event first belonged to a series of choices. When you choose one path from the multitude of possibilities, all of the alternate paths that you did not select continue to exist in parallel worlds.

Here is an excerpt from my journal that resounds with multi-dimensional consciousness:

I retreated to the high red cliffs outside Abiquiu, New Mexico, to empty my busy mind and meditate and be present for beauty. I sat down on the crusty red sand beneath a massive overhanging cliff. I closed my eyes and relaxed on the hard red earth. I began breathing in the dry air. Without warning, I felt overwhelmed with a sense of my own ancientness. Intuitively, I realized that something profound was already in process.

I continued to breathe gently and sent out welcoming energy. In my inner eye, I saw two parallel paths. The first one opened, and I reviewed a lifetime when I was born knowing I was destined to be a healer and serve others. My parents were also healers, as were their parents before them. I was trained by many skillful teachers. As I settled into the energies of that lifetime, I felt a sense of deep love, contentment, and a profound sense of belonging to the community. My growth and development happened without incident or drama.

The second parallel path that opened before my inner eye revolved around my not knowing who I was or what gifts I brought to my family or the world. I was born intuitive and empathic and belonged to a family of rational people. I worked hard to belong and be loved and struggled with feeling isolated and different. My heart felt like an accordion: opening and closing, opening and closing. Drama, death, deception, debt, depression, and suffering challenged me to keep my heart open. Discovering and much later claiming who I was occupied much of this parallel lifetime.

My body shook and I opened my eyes and returned to ordinary consciousness and the clay cliffs that surrounded me. The awareness that I had volunteered for this challenging lifetime made me sigh, laugh, and cry. I exclaimed, "It figures. Now I understand." I had chosen the path of challenge and change. I'd volunteered. Never again could I pretend I'd been drafted when I became discouraged.

The memory of this past lifetime choice reinforced my understanding that we each choose, while we reside in Spirit, the kind of life experiences we need to expand our soul's expression. No question that I have strengthened my will and learned about the importance of discernment this lifetime.

Seventeen years later, I review the above story in amazement because my present life now feels like it has become the first path of healing, ease, and belonging. Synchronicity happens daily, and my soul feels like a magnet that attracts others who are on a spiritual journey and seek further clarity or healing. In my experience, the two separate lifetimes have merged.

"Every time we access multidimensional thinking, we amplify our capacity to become manifesters of our own lives," Chris Griscom, author of *Ecstasy Is a New Frequency*, writes. "I invite you to think of a human being as a multidimensional being made up of divine energy, spirit, heart, mind, emotions, and body who functions in many different contexts of reality simultaneously."

Quantum thinking takes into account both negative and positive probabilities. This year I made a New Year's resolution to practice loving awareness. I challenged myself to be aware of love no matter where I was or with whom. The hymn, "Surely the Presence of God Is in This Place" hummed in my heart. I also committed to extending love to myself. Along with my choice existed doubts and anxieties, as well as a personal history of failing to manifest New Year's resolutions for longer than two weeks. This year I updated my New Year's intention to include both polarities since everything coexists. My intention read: "I will excel in extending loving-kindness to myself and all the people I meet, even though I do not understand how I will accomplish this goal." I do know from my experience that each choice that we make influences the probability of future choices.

Here's a story about a time when quantum thinking challenged each of us:

I was deeply touched when I worked with a friend whose daughter had died seven years ago. I was surprised to discover that they did not have a soul agreement during this lifetime. However, after the daughter's death they crafted a mutual soul agreement. I do not know who initiated the contract, and perhaps it does not matter. Mom agreed never to abandon her daughter, even after her death. She had also agreed to feel how craziness had taken over her daughter's consciousness.

The daughter agreed to receive her mother's love for her, which she seldom had done when she was living. Neither woman had any clue that merging their energies would create cellular insanity in the mother's energy field. Cancer resulted. The daughter had no clue how masterful her mom was at merging. She apologized for the unforeseen cancer and energetically told her mother she was impressed by her mastery. She had not known her mother was a healer. I saw tears in the mother's eyes. She had waited all her life to receive a compliment from her daughter.

The contract was complete. I asked her whom she would trust with her daughter's spirit. She did not know if she trusted God.

"Who would you feel comfortable handing your daughter's soul over to?" I asked gently.

She replied, "My mother, father, and my spiritual teacher."

Then she cried, deep grief mixed with leftover tears. She wanted to feel peace and extend that to her daughter. "Release precedes peace," her guides said. She moaned, "Who will I be without her? She was so wanted."

Then she remembered that a few years after she divorced her husband, they had decided to create a completion and release ritual. They had moved on to become friends—so she had first hand experience with the benefits of releasing a loved one.

When she was ready, she let go of her daughter and her part of the soul agreement. More tears clouded our vision. Then to both of our amazement, a large, shimmering angel arrived and stood close behind her.

So close that when she leaned her head back, she felt comforted.

I sat in silence and watched and marveled at the releasing and reclaiming process. Then she said, "This magnificent angel is one of my guides." I nodded.

The power of love and healing along with the continuous cycle of life, death, afterlife, and how our souls continue to be connected after death leaves me almost without words, except for reverence.

Multidimensional Nature of Mind

I listened to a woman client describe her "incomplete soul assignment." She explained that she had worked on a book in her mind for ten years but could not sit down and type the chapters. She had considered hiring a ghostwriter, but handing over her unfinished work for someone else to finish felt wrong. She described herself as "muddled" and "disappointed."

Intuitively, I wondered if her inertia was tied to a past lifetime or perhaps a past lifetime vow. Often asking the question is all that is necessary to open the time portals. The story unfolded as a French lifetime in which she channeled a book on inner liberation. She was passionate about freeing people from whatever bound them: beliefs, people, politics, and/or events. The country's dictators did not want people to think for themselves and they threatened to kill her. She persisted. Then they sent her a porcelain doll with its legs and arms cut off and a knife in its heart. The message was clear. Her children's lives were threatened. She stopped writing. That was still not good enough for the authorities.

They demanded she burn the book in their presence. She fooled them and burned meaningless pages and smuggled the book out of the country on the back of a mule. However, she died before she knew the book was published and secretly circulated. She believed she had failed in her mission. She judged herself and vowed to never write again. Her present day undermining belief is, "Why bother? It will never amount to anything."

We sat in silence, allowing the impact of the vow to move us into the present time and the present challenge. We moved quickly to reclaim compassion and create a self-forgiveness ritual in order to neutralize the spell of the past. Next, she released the vow of never writing again. Reclaiming her passion, courage, power, and perseverance added to her resolve to write and publish her book. When she left, I wondered how many writers in hiding give up because of an unresolved past lifetime.

I agree with Dr. John Lilly, author of *The Center of the Cyclone,* who writes, "It is my belief that the experience of higher states of consciousness is necessary for the survival of the human species." Since we are all multidimensional beings, we have within our genetic blueprint the potential to tap into all of the knowledge throughout time, including the future.

Dimensions and Frequencies

Dimensions correspond to states of consciousness. Each dimension vibrates on a different frequency and corresponds to a precise reality. Since mutuality exists between dimensions, we need to begin to think in terms of and/and rather than either/or. Reciprocity rules. Dimensions are not aligned in a linear fashion. They coexist in different and simultaneous spaces. The only way to distinguish them is through their vibrations. Buddhists extend a thought or the energy of loving-kindness to reach 3,000 universes.

It is possible to discover, remember, and reclaim all aspects of yourself that have been expressed through all your lifetimes and graduate into your spaciousness. Native Americans end all prayers with "all my relations." I have been expanding on their ways and adding to my prayers the words and feelings, "all my relations in all dimensions" as a way of honoring my multidimensional nature.

To live within the frequency of multidimensional reality requires you to stretch both your imagination and your mind. As Jane Roberts, a well-respected psychic, said, "If you think in terms of a multidimensional self, you realize you have many more avenues open to expression and fulfillment." When Buckminster Fuller was asked in an interview, "How do you get in contact with the universe?" he replied, "You must get on the same frequency." Since each of your lifetimes exists simultaneously, it follows that you have the capacity to access all that you have been and learned in the past as well what you will be and learn in the future. In fact, quantum science suggests the existence of many possible futures for each moment in our lives, and each future lies in a state of rest until it is awakened by choices made in the present. Perhaps you can now appreciate the words of Jorge Ferrer, author of *The Participatory Turn,* when he reminds us, "The more human dimensions that actively participate in spiritual knowing, the more creative spiritual life becomes."

Pause for a moment and listen with your knowing heart to this conversation between five-year-old Noah and me:

Rosie: "Noah, are you nervous about singing on the big stage in your first school concert?"

Noah: "Of course not, Grandmom, there will only be human beings listening to us, you know."

Rosie: "Yes, that's right, Noah."

Noah: "Now, Grandmom, if there were aliens mixed in with the humans I sure would be nervous because everyone knows aliens are the best singers in the universes!"

Time and Timelessness

One of the major differences between ordinary consciousness and multidimensional consciousness is a change in how you perceive the nature of time and space. In everyday consciousness, time and space are experienced as fixed realities, whereas, in multidimensional consciousness, time and space are fluid. Albert Einstein reflected on the illusionary nature of time and space when he said, "Time is not what it seems. It does not flow in only one direction, and the future exists simultaneously with the past." In other words, the concept of past, present, and future all existing simultaneously is one of the ways multidimensional consciousness differs from every day, waking consciousness. Our bodies exist in time and our souls exist in timelessness. This dialogue excerpt from a conversation with my Dearly Beloved explores our relationship with time.

Dearly Beloved: You are beginning to glimpse the big picture. Note that all exists inside time. No thing exists outside of time. The future is already here. Now. You are here. Now. All is here. Now. In order to beckon the future, you must let go of all that you are not. Think of this process as a divesting process. Divesting precedes investing. And then, of course, there is reinvesting. To make this more personal, as you are fond of doing, you divested yourself of your righteous, hurt little girl and reached out. Be aware that there is a vast energetic difference between overriding and letting go.

<u>Rosie</u>: Yes. I need to breathe into the immensity as well as the simplicity of all of this. I feel I do not have the right words to explain how I sense that your wisdom is within me.

<u>Dearly Beloved</u>: That is one of the gifts of awakening into consciousness.

<u>Rosie:</u> Thank you for your presence and your guidance.

I was 34 years old when I experienced an awakening to timelessness. A year after my teenage son was electrocuted in the nearby schoolyard, I volunteered to participate in a one-time controlled and supervised LSD experiment because I needed to take drastic action in order to pierce through my resistance to grieving. Dr. Walter Houston Clark, author of *Chemical Ecstasy* and a highly respected theologian believed that acid had the power to open one up to the sacred dimension. I had to write an extensive autobiography before my "trip" and the small, "white sacrament" had been clinically tested and calibrated to my weight.

Instead of releasing the ever-present pain and loss that resided in my heart as I had expected, I encountered my dead son as pure energy. We traveled together through space and time, played, loved, and manifested magic together. Suffering did not exist, only the spirit of celebration existed. My epiphany came when I experienced his death as one event in a long chain of lifetimes. Time expanded into multidimensionality. For weeks I giggled each time I used the past or future tense of a verb. It took me years to integrate the mystical dimension that I experienced during my twenty-four hour journey.

I had nothing in my life to compare my experience to. Certainly, I had transcended any fear I had of dying, because I experienced the reality that we are energy beings and energy does not die. Surrendering to the multidimensional experience was not an issue, because I knew in advance that I could not control the acid.

To add another layer to the multidimensional ways of knowing, we can overlay past and future lifetimes, as well as parallel lifetimes. To wrap your knowing heart around this concept, imagine you are at a drive-in movie that has three screens. On one screen is a movie of your past, on the neighboring screen is a movie about your present, and on the third screen is a movie about your future. Now imagine that the three movies are playing simultaneously. To add another layer of complexity to our multidimensional model, imagine that superimposed on the original three movie screens are three more screens that include past lives, parallel lives, and future lives that are synchronized with the original three films. Is it any wonder that our normal human mind compartmentalizes our experience to include only our present physical reality?

Akashic Records and DNA

Your personal akashic records contain your individual history, including your spiritual history. Everything that has ever happened to you is recorded on this cosmic internet. Your accomplishments as well as your unfinished business—karma—coexist.

Listen in on a conversation with my guides as I began wrapping my arms around the principles of the akashic records:

Rosie: If providing information for this book were all I had agreed to do, the assignment would be easier. It's the personal work of clearing, claiming, grounding, and living the principles that challenges me.

Guide: This assignment is much more than the gaining of knowledge or loving in the abstract. Speaking, living, embodying, and writing from a spacious heart invites wisdom. Your words transmit a specific wavelength that embodies akashic blueprints. No, you are not on a crusade. You are on assignment as an agent of evolutionary consciousness. Healing results.

According to the principle of quantum resonance, the past still influences us. Information about your soul purpose, soul qualities, karmic imprints, past and future lifetimes are encoded in your DNA. According to Lee Carroll who channels Kryon, in a chapter in *Transition Now*, DNA carries your ancestral and racial imprints, strengths, natural abilities, and hereditary diseases. Your subconscious mind reads and reacts to this information. Your higher self also resides in your DNA.

We are just learning that DNA, which was discovered in 1953, responds to intention and reprogramming. Your personal beliefs and the feelings and emotions surrounding each one can directly change your DNA. Each molecule of DNA, which is a loop, has billions of chemicals within it. Geneticists have discovered that up to 97% of DNA is unused, which they label "junk DNA." Some people believe the blueprint of the future may be contained in the "junk DNA."

Dr. Bruce Lipton, author of *Matter and Miracles*, proved that the DNA nucleus is not the brain of the cell; rather the intelligence center of the cell is the membrane. The membrane receives signals from our unconscious and writes the DNA code. He proved we could actually reprogram our DNA if we are dissatisfied with the blueprint and then broadcast a new message about ourselves to the universe.

The Return of Karma

Karma is another dimension of multidimensional consciousness. The Sanskrit word for karma means "action." Everything that happens to you from the time you are born until you die gives you an opportunity to resolve your karma. Think of karma as a teacher who points out what aspects of your life are out of balance or unfinished. In the School of Love, we learn that the purpose of karma is to integrate the teachings we need in order to open our hearts.

John Lilly believes that karma is anything that continues to take you away from the positive experiences. Karma, like personal limited beliefs, restricts your freedom of choice, compromises your creative process and diminishes your sense of authenticity. Another way to wrap your knowing heart around the concept of karma is to understand the meaning of the esoteric phrase, "As within, so without." How you treat yourself and others creates karma. Thus, karma puts the emphasis on right living.

The principle of karma states that every thought, word and deed has consequences. Karma can compromise the life lessons that are part of your destiny. Once we learn the lesson and make a positive choice, the situation does not recur because our spirit is no longer attached to the negative choice that gave rise to the lesson. Look at it this way: karma allows you to actively shape your past, present, and future based upon your thoughts, words, and deeds. Listen to the wise words of Jerome Washington:

"When I embrace my karma

As I embraced my deeds

Waterfalls become quiet ponds."

Another way to understand karma is to imagine it as pre-programmed consciousness. Many people believe that how you see yourself is a direct reflection of your karma: Karmic patterns are etched in our subconscious mind, which is much larger than our conscious mind and records both experiences and interpretations in the form of feelings. When you wrap your knowing heart around remembering that the mind is conditioned to replicate your patterned ways of seeing, thinking, feeling, and behaving, lifetime after lifetime, it seems logical that you might repeat and reinforce karmic patterns which cause you to suffer. Since karma co-mingles and interacts with mind, it is difficult to identify your own karmic patterns because it is the nature of karma to restrict access to the mind.

If you are motivated by your ego mind, you are likely to reinforce the essential karmic patterns that cause you to suffer. However, there is hope because the same mind that generates and holds the karmic patterns is the mind that can be trained to recognize and release karmic patterns of projections. Suffering lifetime after lifetime is not the purpose of karma. Karma is meant to be resolved, not accumulated. According to John Lilly, "Burning karma is making conscious the consequences of your past actions without shame, anger, or censoring." The process of releasing karma is taking responsibility for your past actions or inactions. In addition, releasing karma can affect the future personality as well as the past one. The year I lived at Findhorn, an intentional spiritual community co-founded by Eileen and Peter Caddy, the two best selling flower remedies were Karma Clear and Manifestation. In reality, the expression of love, gratitude, and forgiveness clears karma.

It is important to note that working on karmic issues does not automatically wipe your akashic record clean. It does increase your freedom to be present in the here and now and neutralizes the issues that originally created the karmic grooves in your consciousness.

Empowerment requires transformation of all karma. It is essential to observe, review, assess and release karma from a witness state that is free of ego. Why? To the extent that you judge, censor, blame, or shame yourself, you create a deeper karmic groove that acts like quicksand to entrap you.

Arthur Osborn, author of *The Expansion of Awareness: One Man's Search for Meaning in Living*, asks us to consider past lifetimes as alternate present lifetimes. He urges us to remember "the reincarnational structure is a psychological construct. The reality of your past lives exists simultaneously with your present life and the distance between one life and another exists only psychologically and not in terms of years or centuries." My experience convinces me that remnants of past lifetimes exist in our emotional energy field. It is always my feelings that alert me to a past lifetime memory, especially when the emotions I am experiencing seem to have nothing to do with my present lifetime reality. He insists there is a constant interaction between you and your reincarnational selves. Look for repetitive themes or distinctive personality characteristics or life orientations for clues to karmic patterns."

I recommend a technique that I call "Peel Away" to release past lifetimes that are not in alignment with your present soul purpose.

❖ Before going to sleep, set an intention to recall and release any former lifetimes that are not in alignment with your soul purpose this lifetime. Remember to send out your gratitude in advance.

The first time I tried this strategy I dreamed of a time when I was drugged by injection to forget everything I knew about teaching people to enter the future via time traveling. Amnesia took over. Before using the Peel Away technique I had no clue that I knew how to time travel, and the idea of teaching people how to travel in time felt like a fantasy, at best.

Karmic Bleed-Through Lifetimes

A karmic bleed-through occurs when the effects of a karmic pattern or cause in a past lifetime erupts in the present. Think of the attraction functioning like an energetic magnet. A similar energetic correspondence in this lifetime fits like Velcro to events or people from a past lifetime. An energetic resonance is experienced in the present. How is this possible? Remember that every single event in all your lifetimes is stored as an energetic imprint in your subconscious mind. Often free will becomes a hostage. People describe the bleed-through as being under a spell or in a trance. Your behavior is no longer under conscious control, but takes on the repetitive pattern of the past lifetime.

Here's another example of a time when I experienced a past life bleed-through. Remember as you read, the opportunity for a breakthrough is always present during a bleed-through experience.

When I was vacationing in Cyprus, I decided to learn how to snorkel. I am a good swimmer and enjoy being in the ocean. However, when I put the facemask on, I panicked. I told myself that my terror was unreasonable, especially since I was standing in shallow water. But I was convinced that I would drown if I put my masked face in the water. My terror overwhelmed me as I ripped the facemask off and ran to shore.

Fortunately my partner was familiar with past lifetime overlays and he gently guided me to review the origins of my fear of drowning. As I remembered the time of forced drowning, I was not surprised to see how a wooden facemask had been over my face to stop me from breathing.

The panic and terror that I had felt earlier was definitely connected to this experience in my distant past. I made the choice to release the strong emotions and free myself to be more fully present for the experiences of this lifetime. Using my intention and breath, I created a boundary between dying by drowning in the past and enjoying snorkeling in the present. I knew I had cleared the trauma when I replaced the facemask and dove into the water. Snorkeling continues to be one of my favorite aquatic activities.

I continue to be surprised and a bit in awe of the paralyzing effects of a past lifetime. When I was immersed in the former lifetime, I felt like I had amnesia because I could not for the life of me connect with being the competent swimmer I am in this lifetime. In addition, when I was seized by the emotions of the former lifetimes, I could not take in the repeated reassurances that my partner gave me. Nothing quelled my fears that drowning was imminent until I realized I felt like I was in a trance—responding as if I had been hypnotized. When I became aware that I was not acting like myself, I began to catch on.

Often we feel an energetic affinity or a resonance with people who share a similar karmic imprinting. Sometimes these people trigger our unfinished karma by mirroring and giving us an opportunity to work through our unfinished business. Whenever you are in the midst of a bleed-through lifetime, take a deep breath, and say "Thank you for this opportunity to free myself." You may have to say it more than once. Without exception, each time you release a karmic program, you release that aspect of yourself that has been imprisoned. Empowerment results from resolving and integrating the trauma of the past.

Benefits of releasing karma include:
- A quieter mind
- Easier access to essence self
- Increased emotional, mental and spiritual freedom
- More trust in self, others, and the universe
- Greater capacity to give and receive love
- Heightened creative expression
- Increase in compassion and forgiveness

Creating Kind Karma

Personally, I do believe in kind karma and have experienced it several times during this lifetime. For example, have you met someone and known instantly that you could trust your new friend? Have you experienced kindness from another person and been unable to figure out why this person was being so generous toward you?

❖ Make a list of people who have extended kind karma to you.
❖ Make another list of people who you have gifted with kind karma.

Based on my experience, kind karma results from honoring one another. A few years ago I committed myself to rebalancing the karma I had created in the past and making a conscious decision to create as little karma as possible for the remainder of my life. I confess I desired to create no more karma, but I decided to avoid setting myself up for the impossible. If you want to clear karma, I suggest adopting the following guidelines:

• Be responsible for your thoughts, words, actions, and behavior.
• Be honest and clear with yourself and others.
• Release grudges.
• Avoid power struggles.
• Move on when the energy feels like it is dying.
• Appreciate and celebrate the differences between women and men.
• Specialize in letting go and forgiveness.
• Identify your unique form of spiritual service and go to work.
• Express gratitude daily.

As a bonus point for opening up to the expanded possibilities that emerge within multidimensional consciousness, consider the guidance of Seth, channeled by Jane Roberts: "What you love will also be part of your experience in this lifetime and others." Trust your guides and teachers to help you grow in love. It is part of their job. Happy loving!

Reflective Consciousness Questions

• How would your consciousness be different if you believed that you were knee deep in grace?
• What would a multidimensional experience be like for you?
• What, if anything, stops you from doing the necessary work to transform your life?
• What counts for your boldest intention this lifetime?

- How do you define power?
- What gives meaning to your life?

Awakening Reflection Responses

I invite you to reflect on the Consciousness chapter and record your insights for this day.

- ❖ I Learned_____
- ❖ I Relearned_____
- ❖ I Discovered_____
- ❖ I Rediscovered_____
- ❖ I Regret_____
- ❖ I Appreciate_____
- ❖ Right Now I Feel_____
- ❖ And I Will_____

Journaling Prompts

Here are a few prompts to give you more to wrap your all-knowing heart around. Feel free to agree, disagree, make your own connections, or write your own quotations.

"Magic is the art of changing consciousness at will." Starhawk

"What is the soul?" someone asked Rumi. "Consciousness," he replied. Rumi

"We must raise our young so they grow up fearless in the face of the tentative." Bob Samples

"The evolution of consciousness is the very essence of spiritual growth." Scott Peck

Intentions and
Manifestations

Chapter Four

Intention and Manifestation: Double Majors

"Intention is a seed of consciousness by which spirit transforms itself into material reality."
- David Spangler

Awakening Our Intention

Like love, we all have an idea of what intention means. I think of intention as a purposeful plan, empowered by will and desire, to perform an action that will lead to a desired outcome. Intention acts like a tuning fork that, when struck, causes other tuning forks to resonate with the same frequency. Our lives mirror our intentions. Whatever we believe in our inner world, we will manifest in the outer world. If we seek to awaken our all-knowing hearts and empower ourselves, we must excel at manifesting our intentions. Gary Zukav reminds us, "Every intention sets energy into motion whether you are conscious of it or not."

Intention as Magnet

Before you manifest anything, your intention first exists as a thought. Thought is living energy. To think is to affect. Each thought we create enhances, depletes, or is compatible with our life force energy. Thought is governed by intention. Lynne McTaggert, author of *The Intention Experiment,* writes, "Intentionality appears to produce an energy potent enough to change physical reality." We are responsible for creating our present reality by controlling the energetic frequency of our thoughts. Make sure your ideas match your psychic intent. To me, thought and love are the most powerful forces in the universe.

Reality changes in the presence of focused intention. Deepak Chopra reminds us, "Consciousness responds to attention and intention. Attention activates the energy field and intention activates the information field, which causes the transformation." We shape our future by how we imagine it. The more focused your intention, the greater the chance of success, because the law of attraction dictates that we attract what we focus upon. We must acknowledge our present reality and take responsibility for creating the life we are living before we can transform it.

❖ I invite you to do a personal manifestation inventory.
- Take a breath and breathe into your high heart.
- Make it your intention to review the last year.
- Focus your attention on identifying the people you have attracted or repelled during the most recent year.
- Next, focus your attention and identify the events and experiences you have attracted or repelled.
- Write about what you desire to manifest in your life now.

The Power of Focused Intention

Clear intention serves as a magnifying glass that gives you a new lens through which you can make a perceptual choice. Caroline Myss, author of *Sacred Contracts*, writes, "Thoughts and intuitions are expressions of energy that move at the speed of light."

Intention has a dual function: attracting and screening. For example, in the nineteen months that I devoted to writing this book, I created a daily heart-centered intention to write, then organize, edit, and finally to publish it. My heart-centered intention focused my energies and at the same time screened out many distractions that might have brought me initial pleasure but no lasting satisfaction.

❖ This strategy will help you to clarify your intentions:
- Divide paper into three columns.
- Label column one "What I don't want"
- Label column two "What I do want"
- Label column three "Why I want it"

- After you reflect on your answers, take action.

Here is a true story of practicing intentional manifestation, which I sometimes call "femifestation."

Years ago, I decided to change my last name. It felt empowering to choose my own name, but I frustrated myself for a few weeks trying to use my logical mind to figure out a name that would remind me of my spiritual path and carry me into my future. As a student of numerology, I knew the vibrations I wanted my new name to carry, but I couldn't find the right letter combination. Finally, I surrendered to my dreams since I knew from experience that dreams tend to bring gifts from my intuition.

The naming dream arrived during the early hours of the morning, telling me my new name: Rosalie Deer Heart. I awoke excited and committed myself to live into the dynamic truth of my new name. Deer Heart resonates with love and compassion for myself as well as others. The name also feels aligned with self-honoring, integrity and service. But the naming story does not end here.

Fast forward to my day in court when a judge would decide whether I could legally use my new name. I thought I was prepared for the judge's questions because my lawyer carefully rehearsed me before my court appearance. Listen in on the conversation:

Lawyer: The judge will ask you, "Have you ever used the name you are petitioning for?"

Rosie: Does that include past lifetimes?

Lawyer: Please answer, "Yes, Your Honor." Then the judge might ask, "Has anyone addressed you by this name?"

Rosie: Do my dream guardians count?

Lawyer: The proper response is, "Yes, Your Honor, my professional colleagues are already using my new name."

As the time approached, I was nervous that one man held my future name in his hands. The judge called me down to the front of the courtroom and looked down at me from the bench.

Judge: "The name you are proposing is an unusual name.

I gulped and said, "Yes, Your honor."

Judge: Has anyone addressed you by this proposed name?

I breathed fast, delighted that I knew the right answer, and replied, "Yes, Your Honor, my professional colleagues are addressing me as Rosalie Deer Heart."

Judge: I have one last question.

I gasped before he elaborated, not knowing what the correct response was supposed to be and nervous that I was so close to having my spiritual name. Yet there were no guarantees.

Judge: Why this name?

He looked directly into my eyes. Without a pause, I returned his gaze and said, "Your Honor, this name honors my spirit and reminds me to stay awake on my spiritual journey."

I watched as the judge stood up and hammered his gavel. Then he intoned, "Never let it be said that I stood between a woman and her soul. Your petition for a name change is granted."

Without a pause, I clasped my hands in front of my heart and bowed to him. To my amazement, he returned the bow. Then my lawyer hurried me out of the courtroom.

Later that day, after celebrating with friends, I sent the judge a bouquet of flowers and signed my new name for the first time. The next day I received a thank you note from him reading, "Rosalie Deer Heart is a perfect name for you. In my 26 years as a judge, this is my first bouquet of flowers." Yes!

Notice I was centered in my heart. I was clear and focused about what I wanted to accomplish, and I knew that I deserved my new name. When I imagined people calling me Rosalie Deer Heart, I felt light, expansive, and connected to my spiritual path.

When we are *not* being consciously intentional, we manifest our unconscious counter-intentions. If we are not in charge of our conscious mind, our unconscious mind will assume control. If we do not believe either consciously or subconsciously that we are worthy of manifesting our dreams, we will attract our fears and limitations

Remember Yoda's instructions to Luke Skywalker in *Star Wars* when he was learning how to levitate objects. When Yoda told Luke to levitate his ship out of the water, Luke said he would try to do it. Yoda told him, "*Do*, or do not. There is no *try*."

Yoda would have approved of the "*doing*" of my five-year-old grandson, Noah. To smile and perhaps be inspired, read the following journal entry that captures Noah's unshakable intention:

"Grandmom, I will find the golden egg at the Easter egg hunt today," Noah announced with passion. It was 5 a.m.

I roused my sleeping body, moaned, "Good luck," and rolled over on my side.

He persisted. "I don't need luck, I know. Aren't you going to ask me how I know? Grandmom? Grandmom?"

I sat up and asked, "Okay, Noah, how do you know you will be the one to find the golden egg and win the big prize?"

He smiled and said excitedly, "My friend, God, telled me, Grandmom."

"Oh," I said, trying to match his enthusiasm.

Later I overheard Noah talking to Malia, "I don't want you to be sad or mad, Malia, because we are in the same age group this year, but even though I am younger, I will win the golden egg."

She shrugged her shoulders, rolled her brown eyes, and said, "Whatever."

Twelve o'clock arrived. About one hundred kids scrambled to claim the hundreds of plastic colored eggs. Everyone except Noah. He stood still, arched his head upward and toward the sky, nodded and walked straight ahead about five feet. He never looked down or reached for an egg.

I began to worry about how he would feel if he did not find the golden egg. Malia returned for another basket and asked, "Why isn't Noah picking up any eggs?" I shrugged. "Does he really think he will find the golden egg with all these kids?"

"I guess he does," I replied.

Together we watched as he cocked his head to the left one more time and listened with the focus of an animal tracker. Then he ran to a big rock, smiled, and struggled to lift the boulder. Then I heard him scream, "Yes!" Kids surrounded him with shouts and high fives.

When he presented the treasured golden egg to me, he said, "See, Grandmom, God said I would find it. And I listened."

Noah exemplified the over-belief principle. He was convinced of a successful egg hunt in which he would win the prize egg. He declared his intention out loud and reinforced his will by repeating his intention. He stayed focused and attuned to his stated goal.

Collaborative Intention

The purposeful enactment of an intention extends beyond the personal into a group intention. Research suggests that the power of intention multiplies depending on how many people are focused on the same objective at the same time. The Transcendental Meditation organization has designed and carried out more than 500 studies of group meditation, which incorporated group intention, to study the effects of meditation on reducing conflict and suffering. The theory is that meditation has a threshold effect. Maharishi believed that if 1% of the population of a particular area meditated with a single intention, conflict of any kind would decrease.

In 1993 TM meditators focused their intention on Washington, DC, from January to May, in what was called TM's National Demonstration Project. Whenever 4000 meditators joined their intentions to decrease violent crimes, the violence decreased. When the experiment ended after 5 months, the crime rate rose again.

❖ I invite you to create a specific, detailed heart-centered intention.

- Engage all your senses. Feel how you will feel when your intention manifests.
- Invite your soul to add its frequency to your intention.
- Smile and send out your gratitude as if you have already succeeded.
- Next, make it your intention to be aware of what you wish tomorrow to look and feel like. Engage in a manifestation walk. Embody how you will feel and look as you manifest your intention.
- Then ask your dream guides to help you to manifest your intention.
- Record your dreams and ask your dream guides for the deeper meaning of your dream.
- When you wake up, repeat or write your intentions for the day.

In summary, imagine that all is within your reach. Everything exists as potential until you activate the energy by your intention. Expect miracles. In other words, the future is already yours. It exists, just as when you visit a restaurant and the server asks, "What would you like?" Intention is the act of placing your order and waiting in exquisite anticipation for your desires to be fulfilled. Carlos Castaneda, author of *The Teachings of Don Juan*, wrote "In the universe there is an indescribable force which shamans call intent, and absolutely everything that exists in the entire cosmos is attached to intent by a connecting link. The universe has a secret. It is responsive to requests."

Manifestation represents the successful results of your intention. Now let's move on to the next class in our School of Love—manifestation, the art and science of creating a future that is in alignment with our all-knowing heart and our soul—and explore how to create the future we desire.

Manifestation as Inner Art

Manifestation is a heart-centered process, and each goal has a specific vibration. No longer is acquiring a new car, or dream home, or fame and fortune the sole goal of manifestation. From the perspective of a knowing heart, it becomes a path of opening up to the preciousness of every moment and responding to it creatively. When we choose to manifest from an all-knowing heart, manifestation is aligned with soul and Being.

Listen to this channeled excerpt from my Dearly Beloved about manifestation:

Dearly Beloved: It is the time to believe in yourself. Believe in the future of the book. Believe in your ability to manifest. All are one in consciousness. Your attitude of "spacious expectancy" is irresistible to the energies of the future, which are, as you are aware, part of your present. Continue to feel fulfilled, because the energy of gratitude invites similar frequencies. Be of an open heart and mind, and the energies of the future will become you.

Rosie: I am ready and waiting without demanding or even longing. I trust all is in divine order—even me!

Dearly Beloved: Yes! And all is well!

Quantum science suggests the existence of many possible futures for each moment in our lives. Each future lies in a state of rest until it is awakened by choices made in the present. When we state an intention, we tell the universe that we are choosing a specific possibility amidst all the available options. Here is a story about a time when I was put to the test in relation to manifestation.

In January 2011, I joined two dear friends—Lou Ann Daly, author of *Human Beings*, and Lynn Potoff, author of *Too Many Skeletons, Not Enough Closets*—in designing a one-day workshop called Spiritual Journeys. Our goal was to treat women to a day filled with networking, shared stories, inspiration, and lightheartedness. The accommodations and meeting rooms were spacious. In order to cover our expenses, we needed to register forty women.

I was challenged since my full time career for the past six years has been as a resident grandmother. I had walked away from my former life, and my outdated mailing list had disappeared when my computer crashed. Even though I challenge myself by asking "what if?" and "why not?" attracting forty women felt like hard work. (Notice the limiting belief.)

Yet I believed in magic—the art of changing consciousness at will—and I appreciated the power of a heart-centered intention. Realizing that I had to be bold, I created an intention to register a minimum of ten women. My affirmation included both aspects of an intention—the vision as well as my not knowing how it would happen. It looked like this: "Thank you for attracting and registering women who are ready to benefit from our teaching and adding to our evolutionary community, even if I do not know how all this will happen."

Within an hour, my phone rang, and a sculpting buddy whom I had not heard from in six years surprised me by asking "What's going on, I finally located you on the Internet." Next, a realtor whom I had lost track of e-mailed me and asked the same question. Within a couple of days, eight more women from my pre-grandmother life checked in. A few of them reminded me of the depressed economy and were concerned that we would lose money. I did not take part in their fear-based thinking. I continued to affirm a successful workshop, and I was amazed with the ease and grace that made the workshop a reality. Creating an intention from an open heart felt like magic.

Manifestation as Teacher

"Manifestation at its heart is about the relationship to ourselves, to the sacred and to the world around us," writes David Spangler, author of *Everyday Miracles: The Inner Art of Manifestation*. The manifestation process transforms you. You have to connect with your high heart in order to know what it is you wish to become.

When your actions are motivated by love, your energy multiplies and accumulates. The surplus energy you gather and enjoy can be channeled to create anything that you want. The Buddha said, "When you fix your heart on one point, then nothing is impossible for you."

❖ To determine whether a goal is in alignment with your soul frequency, take a gentle breath and imagine you have made a specific choice.

- As a result of your choice, do you feel lighter, expanded, excited, and filled with enthusiasm?
- If you respond "yes," you are aligning with your essence.

Manifestation requires a combination of awareness, vision, intention, and action. Experiments show that the focus of our attention changes reality itself and suggests that we live in an interactive universe. You have to experience inwardly what it is that you wish to manifest outwardly.

David Spangler outlines essential questions to ask yourself before making a declaration to manifest:

- Why do I wish to manifest this?
- Does my manifestation goal align with my soul purpose?
- On a scale of 1 to 5, how much do I desire to manifest my goal?

The strength of your desire is one element that determines the success or failure of your project. You may, for example, wish to manifest money to pay off a debt. Visualize being debt free. Activate the energy of over-belief by engaging your emotions and will to the edges of your capacity. How will you feel about yourself when you succeed? How will you feel about your future? Remember to involve your body, mind, and spirit in your exploration. Remember to write out your goals. Research tells us that writing out our goals motivates us to take action, thus making it more likely to achieve them.

On a practical note, practicing being more generous with others puts your intention into action and alerts your unconscious that you trust yourself and the universe. The law of attraction does not discern whether you are pretending, remembering, visualizing, or daydreaming when you energize a thought. It simply responds to your vibrations moment to moment. And the good news is that it can only respond to one vibration at a time!

Here is a first hand story about the power of intention and manifestation:

For a month I have meditated and affirmed beauty, both the beauty of nature and my inner beauty. Knowing that affirmations build consciousness, I do my best to be present as beauty unfolds.

I greet the beauty of each day by waking early and walking outside on the Eastern Promenade, which overlooks a small beach and the ocean. I continue my meditation on beauty as I walk. Today an unshaven, disheveled older man who was retrieving returnable bottles from a large garbage bin interrupted me. I felt impatient and somewhat repelled by him. Then I felt compassion for him and wondered how life had turned him into a garbage picker.

I continued my early greeting of the sun walk and headed toward my favorite rock near the beach. The sun was beginning to add its warmth to the day. I closed my eyes and began to steady and gentle my breath to enter the stillness of meditation. Breathing softly, I began to remember when I was present for beauty and beauty was present for me.

A gruff voice punctured my stillness. "Nice day, don't you think?

I quickly opened my eyes, remembered that I was alone on the beach, and felt a wave of panic. The man I had spotted earlier stood before me, smiling, with his hands behind his back.

"I have something for you," he said, seemingly unaware that he had interrupted me again.

Right, I thought to myself, you have one of those dirty, empty bottles that you collected earlier this day. For the first time, I looked directly at him and decided he was harmless.

So I closed my eyes and held out my hands. When I opened my eyes, I was holding a fresh, long stemmed rose.

He looked at me and said, "Beauty to beauty," and walked away.

I felt stunned. Tears poured down my face. I don't know if he heard me shout, "Thank you!" I watched him climb into his truck and noticed that amidst assorted bottles and other garbage was a tall, silver pail filled with roses. I smiled and thanked this angel flower man for being a teacher for me for this day.

Margaret Mead wrote, "Never doubt that a small group of thoughtful committed citizens can change the world. Indeed, it is the only thing that ever has." Studies have shown that 2% of the world population is able to sustain their experience of joy regardless of what happens outside of them. I believe that peace is joy resting, and love grounds the process. Swami Satchidananda says that we can change the world if everyone had one loving thought a day. Imagine the impact on the world we could have if 4% or 10% of the people consistently held an intention of peace. My friend Peg Brown and I have a vision of inviting the grandmothers of the world and their grandchildren to share their art and visions of peace. We will create a book of practical peacemaking and peacekeeping ideas. The proceeds of the book, *We Are Peace*, will be donated to grass roots peace organizations around the world. In addition, we plan to have a daily worldwide peace meditation to practice collective manifestation. To add your voices and visions to our practical manifestation project, visit my website at www. heart-soul-healing.com.

I have discovered two keys to manifestation: celebrate what you want to see happen more often and expect miracles. Savoring an experience deepens your emotions and creates a green light in your consciousness to attract even more events to celebrate. As we master the art and science of manifestation, we begin to intuit that there are other dimensions at play in our personal consciousness as well as in the universe.

What would happen if you focused your intention on the development and ripening of your intuition? What do you imagine you might manifest? Read on to connect love, intention, and manifestation with growing your intuition.

Reflective Intention and Manifestation Questions:

- What counts for your boldest intention in this lifetime?
- What intentions are you willing to make right now that align you with your high heart?
- Who are your manifestation mentors and how does each one encourage you to embody your vision?
- If you mastered the art of manifestation, in what ways would your life be different?

Awakening Reflection Responses

I invite you to reflect on the Intention and Manifestation chapter and record your insights for this day.

- ❖ I Learned_____
- ❖ I Relearned_____
- ❖ I Discovered_____
- ❖ I Rediscovered_____
- ❖ I Regret_____
- ❖ I Appreciate_____
- ❖ Right Now I Feel_____
- ❖ And I Will_____

Journaling Prompts

Here are a few prompts to give you more to wrap your all-knowing heart around. Feel free to agree, disagree, make your own connections, or write your own quotations.

"Intention orchestrates infinite possibilities." Deepak Chopra

"The rose is itself and the bees come." Swami Satchidananda

"Sometimes the process of manifestation involves taking the pain and learning to transform it into art." Rick Jarrow

"Only when you are deeply connected to your heart can you know its desires. When you are fully present and able to hear your Inner Voice, are you able to consciously know your intention." Lou Ann Daly

"When you undertake a manifestation project, you are heightening and focusing a creative process, like using a magnifying glass to focus sunlight to produce a concentrated beam." David Spangler

Section Three

The Three Sisters and the Sacred Spiral

Intuition

Chapter Five

Intuition

"A commitment to awakening intuition is a commitment to truth."
- Frances E. Vaughan

Awakening to Intuition

I have been a practitioner of accessing my intuition for almost 35 years. To me, intuition is my inner voice of Spirit and I treat it as a highly skilled consultant. I agree with Shakti Gawain, author of *Creative Visualization*, when she writes, "Every time you do not follow your inner guidance, you feel a loss of energy, a loss of power, a sense of spiritual deadness."

In my life, I have noticed that my Aha! insights were delivered through my intuition. As I intentionally courted it, I noticed I became more loving. It took me years to realize that love empowers intuition. If you wish to jump start your intuition, practice loving.

Intuitive awareness is more a process of spiritual unfolding and discovery than acquiring a set of skills. My favorite definition of intuition belongs to Walter Russell who writes, "Intuition is the language of light through which man and God intercommunicate." If you learn to listen, your inner voice will speak to you about your soul's path.

Intuition and Consciousness

Another way to wrap your all-knowing heart around intuition is to think of intuition as a higher form of vision. Etymologically, the word "intuition" is related to vision and means, "to see within." Each time we access our intuition, we tap into the universal mind, which exists in holographic form. Buckminster Fuller, author of *Operating Manual for Spaceship Earth*, was fond of referring to his intuitive thoughts as "remote cosmic transmissions."

Intuition has levels of awareness that range from ordinary to super-ordinary, and its quality depends mainly on our state of consciousness. Higher consciousness is defined metaphorically as the ability to direct attention to the deeper levels of mind. Ordinary intuition includes common experiences like knowing someone will call right before the phone rings, knowing that if you go to a specific place, you will encounter someone you know, or knowing some specific event is about to happen.

Surveys of the American adult population report that 66% say they have had an experience of extra sensory perception such as an accurate intuition about the wellbeing of someone who is away. Super-conscious intuition is more rare and impersonal. The recipient feels the interconnectedness of all or discovers a universal principle that is accompanied by a feeling of awe. When was the most recent time you experienced a deep intuitive connection to the cosmos? It doesn't matter how fleeting the experience, an intuitive connection is a unitive experience.

Ever since I was a little girl, I have been intuitive. My parents nicknamed me "Weenie Witch" because I knew things before they happened. They were mostly simple things, like when the phone would ring and who would be on the other end, or when someone would drop in unexpectedly. On a more practical note, I graduated from college with honors in three years because I knew what questions to study before the exams.

Since junior high school, Egypt has fascinated me, especially the pyramids. I read books about Egypt, collected post cards from Egypt, and dreamed about the Egyptian desert. When I heard about a women's group embarking for Egypt, I took out a loan and signed up for the two-week journey. My intuition woke me up one night before the trip with a clear message. I was to extend my stay for one week. Besides keeping the seven days open, no other information came—not even a suggestion about making a hotel reservation. I knew this was a test, or perhaps an initiation. I also knew I had been waiting for this experience for a long time, even though I could not articulate why. Intuitively, I knew surrender was the theme.

On the first of the seven days, I arrived at the ticket booth with my suitcase in hand. I had purchased tickets here many times before with the group, but this time I was alone. I planned to re-visit the Great Pyramid and await my intuition's counsel. It was early morning and already there was a line at the ticket booth. As I questioned myself about what was I doing, I heard a loud voice say, "I so glad you back. What you need to see to remember?"

I thought he was speaking to someone in front or in back of me. Then he put his hand on my shoulder and I noticed the tears in his eyes. "It is you. I so happy. Where you stay? I take you home to be home with me and my family." Then he picked up my suitcase and hollered to someone to take over his job in the ticket booth.

I felt excited, nervous, and a bit skeptical. Although some might describe me as naïve, I had experienced the common past life pickup line already a few times in Egypt. However, this time felt different.

"I so happy you come back. I be happy to help you remember. What can I show you? I have the keys to any places you want to go. I show."

He disappeared back to the ticket booth. I reminded myself to breathe and gulped some water.

He returned, put out his hand and said, "People here call me Champion."

During the week I heard many stories of how my guide entertained royalty and people from all over the world by running to the top of the pyramid and down in less than nine minutes. This is a remarkable feat that has not been duplicated, even by his two sons.

Three places attracted me. The first was a tomb that had been locked during my first visit. "No problem, I have keys," boasted Champion. "I unlock and you visit. Maybe you remember."

I also wanted to revisit the Great Pyramid at night. Champion arranged an overnight visit, and I sat near the sarcophagus and had vivid dreams but no remembering. He also escorted me to the pit of the pyramid, a dark and smelly place that held no memories for me, though I had been told it did for others.

The third pyramid, which I nicknamed the Baby Pyramid, somehow felt like home to me. Champion promised me he would give me the keys to that pyramid when I "remembered." Each night he and I ventured out of the compound where hundreds of families lived adjacent to the Sphinx, and I meditated on the paws of the Sphinx from about two to four a.m. He would whistle and I would return his whistle, and then he walked me home. I slept in his red sitting room where he had received so many people and told them stories. He slept on the floor outside my door, which he locked from the outside. No escaping this time!

Five days passed, and I had a few glimpses of past lifetimes but nothing stuck. Finally Champion suggested we rent three donkeys, ride a few miles into the desert, and stay there all night within sight of the pyramids. When I reminded him that camping out in the desert was illegal, he said, "No problem." We loaded the saddlebags with water, hard-boiled eggs, fruit and charcoal to keep the coyotes at bay and took off as the sun was setting. We also slung blankets over the donkeys' backs because the desert gets cold at night.

We prayed for me to remember. Champion told me he was not allowed to tell me what he knew of our shared history. It was my job to remember. I sensed he both wanted me to remember and was also anxious, and I shared similar feelings. Yet I was aware that my time to remember was closing, and I wanted to know everything. We built a small fire and prayed together. As darkness surrounded us, the pyramids seemed to disappear. I tried to keep a picture of them in my mind to attract memories, but I fell asleep. Sometime during the remainder of the night, I remembered a past lifetime. Champion and I were raised to be "antennas" and to direct people to places that amplified their knowing. He was older than I and was responsible for training me. We did this as a service to people. However Champion became greedy and decided to charge exorbitant amounts of money to direct seekers. I disagreed and threatened to expose him to the authorities.

He laughed saying, "Who would believe you? I am your teacher. Besides you are a woman."

I was outraged. I knew our work was sacred, and I also knew that demanding money was wrong. I watched the past lifetime go by like a movie. I appealed to the authorities. Champion won, as he predicted, and I was exiled. I returned to my beloved pyramids only during dreamtime. I never saw Champion again and we both grieved. At last I understood why he was so excited to see me once again. He wanted to make amends and bring peace to the karma of the past. I felt grateful to him for taking me to the desert so I could remember.

When we awoke, he chuckled as I told him the lifetime I remembered. Then he told me there were several others almost the same but maybe I did not have to remember "every bead."

"What you want now?" he asked seriously.

I hesitated to ask if I had remembered enough to gain the keys to the third pyramid. Instead I said, "More than anything, I want to guide people to the places that trigger memories for them again. I want to do that with you like we did before."

He nodded. I reached for his hand. "Together like before but no charging money."

When we returned to Champion's house, his wife served tea, and he handed me the large silver keys to the third pyramid. Then he said he was tired and he would see me after his nap.

Although it was early morning, women had already lined up at the compound's well to draw their pails of water for the day. Chickens scattered as I walked slowly to the third pyramid. I pinched myself several times to make sure this was happening in real time.

In the distance, I spotted the guard at the door of the pyramid. Before I climbed the many steps that led to the entrance, I noticed the big smile on his handsome face. Like most of the guards, he was tall and muscular and young. I felt excited and a bit embarrassed. What would I say to him about the keys I held tightly in my hand?

Before I figured out my words, I heard myself speaking in Arabic. However, I had no idea about what I said.

His smile widened and he said in perfect English, "Of course you can enter. This is your home. No baksheesh needed. This is your home."

I handed him the large key and he said, again in English, "Do you remember the way?"

Once more I addressed him in Arabic. Again I had no idea what I said.

He moved aside, and I heard him lock the giant door from inside. For about a minute I wondered if I needed to worry about being locked inside a pyramid, but then my feet carried me down the 22 steps to a familiar room. It was dark. I walked to the center of the stone enclosure and was still for a few seconds. Then my body began to move. First my legs, then my arms and hips. The exaggerated movements felt like Eternity moving through me. My eyes were closed. Time was dance. Space was rhythm. The dance bridged time and space. Then I heard notes, actual sounds that my body remembered from long, long ago. The memory of the sounds felt like an ancient soul memory, and I smiled and continued to dance. The deep chanting added to my whirling movements, and I felt like I was creating a trance! Suddenly I opened my eyes. The guard smiled and continued chanting. He nodded and said in English, "Remember I sang and you danced. All to raise the energy and to make big the energies of the pyramids."

My body responded to his words and I knew he spoke truth. I continued my dance, and my movements expanded into sensuous play. No self-consciousness here. Then for a moment I questioned if I was stupid to continue to dance inside a locked pyramid with an unknown man singing and watching me. My heart was open and I dismissed worry. Somewhere from deep inside my body, I understood that I was inside of time and I was realigning with my soul. I felt protected and even graced. I continued to dance to his chants, remembering more about energy amplification with each step.

Without warning, he stopped chanting and I stopped dancing. He said something in Arabic that I did not recognize. We both smiled. Then he took my arm and gently led me up the stairs and out into the piercing desert sunlight. My last memory is of looking into his teary eyes.

Without thinking, I said in English, "You knew."

He replied, "I, too, waiting for you to return. Return the keys back to Champion."

Not until I was walking back to the compound did I wonder how he knew. The sun was high in the sky when I encountered Champion. Without asking if I remembered more during my time in the third pyramid, Champion took me by my arm and said, "Come, we work together as we did before."

"Yes, I like that idea. Thank you," I said with love.

We walked to the ticket booth hand in hand. We waited until the people approached us and asked if we could help them find particular places. Together we guided them to their trigger places of memory acceleration. No charge!

I facilitated spiritual journeys to Egypt for several years, and Champion and I worked together to bring people together with places that accelerated their remembering and knowing. The breakthroughs and the gifts helped to heal all of us.

Intuition as Frequency

Intuition operates on a different frequency than our normal thinking. It perceives wholes, while our every day mind tends to deal with parts. Your intuition visits more frequently when your mind and heart are aligned, and you are relaxed. Quieting the mind is essential for awakening and deepening intuition. According to Dr. Frances Vaughan, author of *Awakening Intuition,* "The regular practice of meditation is the single most powerful means of increasing intuition."

Intuitions are often registered at the level of feelings. Listen to the intuitive advice from Eileen Caddy, author of *Opening Doors Within*, and one of my favorite teachers: "Cease trying to work everything out with your minds. It will get you nowhere. Live by intuition and inspiration and let your whole life be revelation."

The first angel I met was at Findhorn in Moray, Scotland. It is one of the largest intentional communities in Britain and is home to more than 400 people.

While meditating, I was aware of a subtle shift in my energy field. Imagine that your energy field was filled with tiny champagne bubbles. I had no idea what was happening. I only knew that I felt like I was being prepared for something. The quickening of my energy continued for three days. At times I became so attuned and fascinated by the accelerated energy that seemed to combine with mine, that I could not speak.

Seeking an explanation from someone who had dedicated her life to her inner experiences and outer channeling, I visited Eileen Caddy, the co-founder of Findhorn. We sipped tea for an hour before I told her the real reason for my visit. She smiled and reached for my hands. Then she got up and poured us another cup of tea.

"Of course, My Dear, it is perfectly obvious to me. Why did you not visit me sooner? The Angel of Findhorn wishes to speak through you. Welcome her. This is her home, and we all look forward to her visits and her insights."

The next day I channeled an anniversary message from the Angel of Findhorn. I was nervous and had no idea what to expect. I had never channeled an angel before or since. The community welcomed the angel and me, and we enjoyed a lively question and answer session. The angelic energy remained with me for a few days after the event, and I miss her.

Imagination is one of the ways our intuition communicates with our more conscious self. Any time that you deny your imagination, you cut yourself off from your intuition and isolate yourself from the sacred. Imagination is loyal to an expanded consciousness. Rumi captures the essence of imagination in this poem:

Every time you imagine something,
You think you lift the curtain
And find the truth
Your imagination is really your curtain.

Catalysts for intuition include:
- A consciousness aligned with relaxed awareness
- A receptive mind and open heart
- Single minded concentration
- An attitude of non-attachment
- Openness to wonder and playfulness
- An ability to suspend judgment and inquire about the deeper meaning

Roadblocks to intuition include:
- Negative beliefs
- Low self esteem
- Inability to relax and be comfortable in the unknown
- Need to control
- Over dependence on linear thinking

Surrendering To the Call of Intuition

We are not in charge of when our intuition will come calling. During my first walk around Iona, an island of western Scotland in the southern Inner Hebrides, I was attracted to an area that consisted of a few dilapidated buildings. My heart beat faster as I approached the ruins. My legs began to shake, and I rested on a large, nearby stone. Then tears eclipsed my vision. Familiar now with the emotional impact of past lifetime memories, I asked to remember specific details of the lifetime that the ancient edifices had shaken loose. Nothing. My body shook, and my tears became sobs and then moans. I pleaded for insight. No information. My only awareness was a fleeting sense of betrayal, intense emotional and physical pain, and a vague sense of injustice.

I returned to the retreat center with red eyes, chills, and raw emotions. I felt like I had unwittingly punctured a deep wound. Since the other twelve retreatants had agreed on a voluntary seven-day vow of silence, I could not ask anyone about the history of the island. However, I found a book about Iona in the retreat center's library. I held my breath as I learned that the remnants of the building that produced the strong reaction were originally a convent of an order of Benedictine nuns that was established in 1208.

Once more I walked the trail to the convent, determined to break through my resistance and discover the roots of my pain. This time I placed my hands on the rocks. Then I opened my mouth and spontaneously licked one of the stones, hoping for information. Once more tears blocked my vision. Brushing the tears from my eyes, I trudged around the old building, hoping that the earth or the structures would open my memory bank. My body shivered, and I returned to my sitting rock.

Not knowing what else to do, I half closed my eyes and prayed. Instantly, my eyes were drawn to a high part of one of the ruined buildings, and I intuitively knew I had lived in that corner once upon a time. I prayed harder, and as if a movie were playing in front of my eyes, I saw a young nun kneeling in prayer. I studied her and knew from deep within my present wombless body that she was pregnant. The movie fast-forwarded and I watched in fascination and trepidation as a monk denounced her for stealing sacred relics and ordered her body dumped in the harbor. He further decreed that other nuns never speak her name on penalty of being cast out of the order. Instinctively, I understood that the monk, who had sentenced the nun to death, was the father of her child.

Although I did not want to watch her drown, I knew I must re-live the feelings of my innocence and injustice in order to release the emotional memories. I did. No wonder love is complicated and painful for me this lifetime. No wonder I looked clueless recently when a friend said, "My sexuality is part of my spirituality." No wonder spirituality and sexuality feel entangled and unclear for me. No wonder I have left several committed relationships when I realized I had abandoned my soul for the illusion of love. No wonder as a teenager I desired to be cloistered to escape my physical passions. Perhaps once I released this traumatic past life memory, I could heal the inner split between spirituality and sexuality and enjoy a deep, loving, long lasting relationship.

Intuition as Transformation

Duane Elgin, author of *The Living Universe*, believes that each of us has an intuitive connection to the cosmos, even though we might not recognize it, and our intuition may be undeveloped. He believes that following your intuition accelerates transformative experiences. Our intuition provides access to the divine plan that directs our life.

In a typical intuitive experience, we have a sense of being a recipient rather than an initiator. However, in my Awakening Intuition classes, I remind people that reciprocity reigns in your relationship with your intuition. That means we can play "cosmic catch." Experiment with initiating or throwing the ball by intentionally engaging in automatic writing. At other times, simply be open to being the recipient of information or guidance.

I adopted a practice that Barbara Marx Hubbard named Dearly Beloved, in order to play cosmic catch with my guides and teachers. Most of the time, I initiated the flow of wisdom from my Dearly Beloved in an exchange like the following:

Rosie: Dearly Beloved, please guide me in finishing the book. I appreciate your enduring Presence even though I have been missing.

Dearly Beloved: The time is ripe to bring the book to completion. Your motivation is now centered within your knowing heart, and that is essential. It is a paradox, Dear One, that you, who are writing about a knowing heart, took up residence in your mind.

Rosie: Exactly! Last night I worked from an open heart and an open mind, and I had fun!

Dearly Beloved: The frequency of fun leaves you exhilarated and open, and that is one of the ways that emerging evolution plays with you. You are connected with All That Is. Please let that be enough.

Rosie: It's a deal! Thank you.

Dearly Beloved: The pleasure is mine.

I honored our connection by acting upon the guidance. Dearly Beloved often surprised me with "blink truths," as her part in the cosmic catch encounter.

Dearly Beloved: Listen for guidance. Reach out for feedback and weigh it carefully, because the feedback that you receive is a reflection of where others reside in their own consciousness. Ultimately, you make the final decisions based on your consciousness. Believe that you and your words are blessed.

Rosie: If I allowed myself to believe like that, I would feel filled with ease and grace. The many ways I pressure myself would disappear.

Dearly Beloved: As always, the choice is yours.

Rosie: Thank you for the clear guidance and support.

Dearly Beloved: You are most welcome.

Accessing Your Intuition

The first requirement for consciously awakening intuition is a clear intention to access your inner wisdom, or divine potential. Intuition does cut through confusion and deception and exposes truth. However, you must be prepared to release preferences, cherished beliefs, and a desire to hear what you wish to hear.

Intuition functions most effectively in relaxed conditions. Learning to quiet the mind and develop a single pointed concentration focuses our intuition. Accessing your intuition involves trust. First, you must trust yourself to let go of trying to make something happen. The harder you try to gather guidance, the less information you receive. Ram Dass offers a perfect metaphor: "Ambition does to intuition what a weevil does to a granary." You must trust the process. Next, you must trust your guides/teachers/God. Finally, you must trust yourself to take action based on your guidance. Taking action based on your inner guidance builds trust and lets your intuition know that you value it. Intuition is experienced to the degree it is expressed and valued. We can all tap in to intuitive knowledge. Here's how.

Techniques for Accessing Your Intuitive, Knowing Heart

- Relax. Breathe in relaxed awareness. Still your thoughts and expectations. Relax your physical body. Calm your emotions.
- Smile. Remember a time when you were filled with the energies of joy, happiness and celebration. Breathe in the energy of irresistibility.
- Surround every cell in your body with love. Breathe in the love of the universe. Repeat the mantra, "I am love loving."
- Gently move your loving energy to your high heart, the energy center midway between your human heart and throat.
- Imagine you have two lines extending from either side of your head out to the heart of space. Remind yourself that one line is for incoming information and the second line is for outgoing gratitude.
- Affirm your intention to be a channel for God's love.

- Invite your guides and teachers to come even closer and welcome them with love.
- The instant you receive an impression, feeling, word, or knowing, say to yourself or out loud, "The first thing I am aware of is…"
- Take action based upon your guidance.

Sri Gurudev Chitrabhaum wrote, "Knowing is not enough. Risk knowledge with action, and then you will know whether it is genuine, pretension, or just information." I recommend using the following questions to distinguish between intuition and mind chatter:

- Is the information grounded in love?
- Do you feel an inner sense of rightness about the information?
- Does the information expand your sense of self?
- Does the information carry lightness?

If you are aware of doubts, confusion, or anxiety, remember to breathe into your high heart and continue to send out gratitude. Love entrains your intuition and overrides the stress response. "Totem Pole" is a technique I developed to attract a lighter frequency of information. I use it when I feel blocked. Imagine a totem pole that is colored black at the bottom and becomes increasing lighter as you move to the top. To return to clarity, breathe your way up to the pure white top of the totem pole.

Since your intuition connects you to the universal mind, avoid making personal interpretations. Why? They are limiting. Practice asking inwardly, "What is the deeper meaning?" During a soul reading, I received an image of a long-stemmed red rose. I have many personal meanings for roses. However, when I asked for the deeper meaning for my client, I discovered the rose was a symbol for her close friend who was dying of cancer. Once I connected to the meaning, more information opened up.

Listen in on a conversation between my guides and me about irresistibility and attraction:

Guides: Now that you have reclaimed clarity, your energy field is being reconfigured. You are being assisted in remembering.

Rosie: Am I right in remembering that merging is a technique to write about, practice, and teach? Like merging with personal guides, merging with the commitment to be a healing resource for the Source, and ultimately merging with cosmic consciousness?

<u>Guides</u>: Yes, you are refining your understanding. Once you experience the infinite possibilities that make up cosmic consciousness, merging becomes irresistible. The frequency of irresistibility is magnetic and entrains others who are opening to Spirit.

<u>Rosie</u>: I just realized that I have taught all this before. I feel as if I am in a process of retrieving.

<u>Guides</u>: Right! The law of attraction is a reflection of your readiness to be in alignment with your soul purpose.

The Intimate Intensity of Intuition

We all recognize deep truth when we receive it or hear it. We know it in our bones. We know it in our knowing heart. I used to be covered by goose bumps, tiny shivery eruptions on my neck and arms when I was in the midst of truth. I refer to these body signals as "Goddess bumps" as my way of honoring the divine feminine.

My intuition had instructed me about the existence of energy pellets that were like time-release capsules that reside in specific places as well as in the force field of our consciousness. I was intrigued by the theory that we leave behind resources or knowledge or memories in a past lifetime, and in order to reclaim the knowledge, we need to revisit the original place. Less than a year after I wrote about energy pellets, I received an experiential flood of remembering that was much more scary than intriguing.

Intuitively, I knew I needed to travel to Cyprus although I had no idea why. When the plane landed, I felt anxious. I continued to feel anxious for most of the 16 days of our visit. I knew in advance that U.N. Peacekeepers maintained an uneasy peace, but that did not explain the depth of my anxiety.

Several people recommended that we visit a particular castle. Each time someone mentioned that castle, my body tensed and screamed, "No!" We approached the castle twice, and I got physically ill. Then I recognized the depth of my resistance and remembered that I had committed myself to clearing whatever needed to be released in order to claim my sovereignty. Yet every cell in my body urged me to run away.

As soon as my feet touched down on the castle grounds, I felt bereft and breathless. I had no explanation for my raw emotions and I dreaded the drama.

The tour guide was friendly and spoke English. He looked surprised when I told him I needed to visit the third floor where the ladies-in-waiting had resided in the past. He nodded his head and said with a wink, "Most people don't know about that." I felt nauseous as I climbed the stone stairs.

When we reached the top step, I regressed 400 years without warning. Upon entering the room, I witnessed, with my inner eyes, my former 16-year-old attractive self as a lady-in-waiting to the queen. More memories flooded my consciousness. I remembered my ardent vow of faithfulness to my queen as well as how deeply I loved her. As I looked around at the familiar furniture, I also remembered the king, who was 15 years older than his 28-year-old wife. My body shook as I remembered how I kept my distance from him.

I still felt nauseous, and I knew an energetic memory lurked close by. Part of me wanted desperately to remember every single detail of the past lifetime, and the other part of me wanted desperately to return to my normal life. My desire to be whole won out.

I breathed in the energy of the room and asked my guides to unwrap the past lifetime. With the next breath, I was in the middle of the drama. All of the court, with the exception of my queen, was engaged in a hunting party. The king cut me off from the rest of the group and ordered his men to go on ahead. He and I were alone. Although I was young, I was old enough to know his intentions. I screamed for help, but nobody came. I fought him, but he was strong. He raped me and then assured me that he had loved me since the day I arrived in court.

I was devastated because I believed I had betrayed my vow of allegiance to my queen. I told nobody what happened. I convinced myself that nobody would believe me. The king had all the power. Under the cover of darkness, I fled the castle. I dared not return to my family because I convinced myself that I had disgraced them. I wandered for days without food or water. I traveled at night, hiding from the king and his men because he had vowed to pursue me if I ran away. After many lonely months of wandering, I died.

Being a veteran of past lifetime bleed-throughs, I knew what my knowing heart needed in order to reclaim its sovereignty. First, I needed to forgive my former self and surround myself with loving compassion and understanding. I inhaled deeply and exhaled some of the trauma. Again I inhaled deeply and felt the stirrings of compassion in my heart. Next, I felt an urge to remind my queen that I had never stopped loving her. I breathed deeply and allowed my tears to spill over. Letting go of the king's assault was the hardest thing for me to release, and yet I knew I must if I wished to be free. Next, I chose to release all self-blame, loneliness, and fear. When I was done, I felt shaky but more confident. I knew the next step would be more empowering. I breathed into my knowing heart and reclaimed joy, trust in myself and my sexuality, love, and freedom. When I walked down the cement stairway toward the outside, I no longer felt scared or nauseous. Perhaps one day I will remember the castle as a place of liberation.

Up until this moment, the energetic unfinished themes of this past time had clearly played out in my current lifetime. What I realized in Cyprus was the power of self-judgment and shame, and how guilt overpowers self-love. Also, I never imagined that the queen would forgive me or even listen to my story. So I believed that I had no power. The energetic overlays from this past lifetime included giving my power away to men, a tendency to self-judgment and toward remaining silent because I expect I will not be believed, and resisting asking for help when I am in trouble.

Dialoguing With Your Intuition

If your mind is not immediately amenable to moving over and giving your intuition control, you might benefit from creating a dialogue between your head and your heart. I have included a brief example from my ongoing journal.

Remember to shift body positions each time you switch voices.

<u>Heart of Intuition</u>: I am tired of you trying to take over and direct my life. I need you to relax and give me more room.

<u>Head</u>: Why should I? I have more experience than you. My job is being the director.

<u>Heart of Intuition</u>: I am growing up! I trust myself to make choices, and I know that with more experience, I will trust myself even more.

<u>Head</u>: How can you possibly guarantee that? I know which is the right course of action. I know how to defend and control.

<u>Heart of Intuition</u>: I agree. Sometimes proof is experiential. I am more interested in wisdom than knowing. I am more interested in acting from my feelings. I am willing to collaborate. I want to make decisions from a place within my heart. That's where you come in. I want us to collaborate.

<u>Head</u>: Never heard of such a place. Feelings are a nuisance. They create confusion and I have to work hard to gain clarity. No thanks!

<u>Heart of Intuition</u>: (Sigh!) I believe that making a decision based on facts and feelings is the way of clarity. I have no need to replace you. My desire is to grow together. I have waited a long time to feel equal. Now is the time. How about a trial engagement?

<u>Head</u>: And then you will stop badgering me? Okay as long as I get to set how long this experiment lasts.

<u>Heart of Intuition</u>: Agreed. Thank you.

Intuition is an essential course in our School of Love. As Dr. Frances Vaughan reminds us, "With intuitive insight comes self-acceptance, compassion, and love." Creating a relationship with your intuition will definitely expand your perception of who and what you are capable of becoming and being.

I make a practice of consulting my intuition daily. Since I continue to be a hopeless journal keeper, I usually meditate for about twenty minutes, and just as I am returning to ordinary reality, I write, "What do you most wish for me to know, remember, or wrap my heart around?" Then I write "Thank you." Often the guidance comes in what I call "spiritual shorthand." Read the succinct advice below:

Back to authenticity

Back to disempowering old fears

Back to love another as much as you love the Divine

Back to air, earth, fire, and water

My immediate human reaction was, "Oh, no! This guidance sounds like gaining more experience in relationships." And then I surrendered. Sometimes intuition speaks to us in our dreams. Read the following excerpt from a past journal about the insistent nature of my intuition.

I dreamed about a volcanic lake for three successive nights. Upon waking, I remembered the name Crater Lake, but I had no conscious idea where or what Crater Lake was. When I told my friend John about my dreams, he said, "I know where Crater Lake is, Rosie, and I will take you there." No easy task since I was living in Maine, he was living in Colorado, and Crater Lake was in Oregon.

Two months later we arrived at Crater Lake. I started to cry before we parked the car. When I stepped out of the car, my body began to tremble uncontrollably.

As we sat before the lake, I remembered how to jump forward and backward through time. I was grateful to my intuition for delivering the dream as well as reminding me how to travel through time.

A couple of weeks ago, someone mentioned Crater Lake in a conversation, and the memories of my visit flooded me. I was amazed that the lake looked like the same one I had seen in my dreams. I remembered also the cellular feeling of knowing I had lived near this lake before, and that made no sense to me—not until many years later when I learned that the earth guardians are spirits that exist without bodies and watch over specific places on the earth. I believe I was once an earth guardian at Crater Lake, and that explains the powerful emotions that surged through my body when I visited it in this lifetime. "Homecoming" is the best word I can think of to describe the intensity of my feelings.

The Collaborative Power of Intuition

Although we typically think of our intuition as personal, I was privileged to witness group intuition. Some might call this the collective evolutionary impulse. Keep your heart open as you read:

I attended my first Pow Wow today in Taos, New Mexico. A Pow Wow is a sacred gathering of many Indian tribes where children, men, and women compete for dancing prizes as other tribal members sing and beat huge thunder drums.

Excitement rushed through me when the announcer signaled the girls' dance. The drummers began beating the huge thunder drum. The singers began to chant in languages I did not understand. About 20 little girls, ages three to five, entered the circle, nodded to one another, and began to move their moccasined feet to the loud beats of the drum—all except one little girl who stood motionless, desperately looking in the direction of her family. I watched as the rest of the young girls whirled and swirled in time with the drums. For the first few drum measures, none of the girls in the circle noticed the one who did not move. Only her silent tears moved.

People watched, whispered, and pointed in the direction of the little girl dressed in white leather, red beads in her hair, and immaculate, new, white beaded moccasins. Then one of the older girls—she was perhaps five years old—noticed this girl and stopped dancing. As if by a silent command, each dancer stopped abruptly although the loud drumming continued. In one unified, swooping movement, all the girls surrounded the crying girl, creating a wall of protection around her.

The audience stretched their heads closer to the circle, hoping to hear the whispered conversations. The persistent drumming drowned out their words. People began to wonder out loud, "Will they dance? Will she dance? Will everyone be disqualified? What will happen to the money purse? Why don't her parents do something?"

Nobody moved. Nothing seemed to happen for minutes. Then the announcer interrupted the questions and the speculation and in a booming voice proclaimed, "And the winner of the money purse for the girls' competition is…everyone!"

People whooped and whistled. All the little girls clapped and danced circles around one another. The older girls gently led the girl who did not dance back into the open arms of her family. Strangers hugged one another and many cried. My heart opened wide and I felt privileged to witness this heart-centered ritual of community intuition and kindness.

My intuition had the final word as I committed weeks to the final editing process of this book. Read for yourself:

Surround yourself and the book with love. Love the process. Effortless wholeness is the key. Without the churning interference of your mind, the book flows lovingly. Remember the book is a gift of love and it is important to resonate with love's frequency as you edit. Avoid rushing and pushing yourself to figure out every detail all at once. Surround yourself and the final editing process with love. Love the synchronicity and remember that creativity is the keynote.

Reflective Intuition Questions:

- How do you recognize your intuition when it signals you?
- Who are the cheerleaders for your intuition?
- How do you know the intuitive information you are receiving is authentic?
- If you believed that your intuition was the silent voice of Spirit, how would your life be different?
- When you consciously align with your intuition, what do you imagine you are capable of contributing to the evolutionary unfolding of this planet?

Awakening Reflection Responses

I invite you to reflect on the Intuition chapter and record your insights for this day.

- ❖ I Learned_____
- ❖ I Relearned_____
- ❖ I Discovered_____
- ❖ I Rediscovered_____
- ❖ I Regret_____
- ❖ I Appreciate_____
- ❖ Right Now I Feel_____
- ❖ And I Will_____

Journaling Prompts:

Here are a few prompts to give you more to wrap your all-knowing heart around. Feel free to agree, disagree, make your own connections, or write your own quotations.

"Intuition is the place of truth." Amy Ahlers

"Intuition is less about divining the future than it is about entering more authentically into the present." Joan Borysenko

"Your divine potential is the fullest expression of your spirit. It is discovering the depths of your capacity to create and express love, compassion, forgiveness, generosity, and wisdom." Caroline Myss

"Using our intuitive intelligence means being in tune with all of creation, intentionally letting down our guard and allowing ourselves to become open to the infinite possibilities that are available to us in the form of awareness." Caron B. Goode

Being in a committed relationship with our intuition expands our consciousness. We receive information that sometimes astounds us. As we open our hearts and trust our inner guidance, we risk moving beyond the familiar behaviors of our ego. When I was in graduate school, everyone received an epigram to live into during our final year. Mine was, "The less you risk, the more you lose when you win." Clearly, my professors meant for me to move beyond ego identification. My spiritual journey took many years as I peeled back layers of consciousness and embraced other ways of knowing and being. The next chapter explores the key elements of the spiritual journey we are all on, whether we are aware of it or not.

Spirituality

Chapter Six

Spirituality

> *"Spiritual growth is now replacing survival as the central objective of human experience."*
> *- Gary Zukov*

The Lessons of Engaged Spirituality

Spirituality is grounded in the power of love. Love is both a spiritual practice and a required course in our School of Love. When I look around me, I see both the power of love and the love of power. My heart aches when I watch the news on television and nightly see people killing one another. My eyes well with tears when I read about the growing number of homeless people. My mind cannot comprehend that 25,000 people died in an earthquake. My soul is confounded with the lack of spirituality in our political process.

I am sad when I admit to myself that much of the world seems to be ruled by the love of power, because I know that spirituality embodies the power of love, and I believe that deep down inside your all-knowing heart, you know the truth of love too. Like intuition and creativity, spirituality is grounded in love. I look for signs of hope amidst the devastation and chaos. Seeing more and more people awakening to the call of Spirit encourages me, and I know you are one of those because you are holding this book in your hands.

In one of my favorite fantasies, I imagine sitting everyone on this planet down together and reminding all of us why we came here. I say, "Remember that we agreed to learn about love and lead our lives with love." I whisper into the tiny ears of babies, "You are love—remember." I awaken our collective memories and remind us that love connects us to our souls and our souls connect us to Spirit. Then I nurture the awareness that we are all creators, and love is our medium. My spiritual fantasy ends as I inspire everyone to remember that our destinies are forever connected.

There is no one way to prepare for the spiritual journey. We only know that a preparation must be made. I offer the following guidelines, based on my experience:

- Be aware of yourself long enough to know that you are present.
- Examine your motives to determine if they come from your ego or your soul.
- Extend acts of loving-kindness without asking for anything in return.
- Avoid struggles, drama, comparisons, and gossip.
- Discern between sources of toxicity and sources of nurturance.
- Laugh at yourself and the world daily.
- Indulge in enjoyment daily. Take time to savor your experience.
- Commit yourself to one spiritual practice and stick to it.
- Delight God.
- Give from your overflowing cup only.
- Extend a 51% vote to your intuition.
- Polish your soul's favorite form of creativity.
- Expect and identify one miracle daily
- Express gratitude when you wake up and before you go to sleep.

I know that talking about love and living love are different. That is where embodied spirituality comes in. In our School of Love, embodied spirituality is a required course, not an elective. Engaged spirituality is the cultivation of a heart that opens endlessly. Transformation requires that the fullness of the unseen dimension of spirit be lived through our body. Our bodies flourish and become vehicles of experience for our spirit in engaged spirituality. The affirmation, "My body, heart, mind, and soul are balanced, vital, and healthy," radiates the essence of engaged spirituality.

- ❖ To track the inner and outer landscape of your spiritual journey, write your responses to the following soul prompts:
  - Make a list of the times when your heart was most open.

- When did you first hear the call of Spirit and how did you respond?
- What happened to your heart?
- List the bold life changing choices you have made in your journey. For an extra challenge, list your decisions in five-year increments.
- What does your heart need in order to open more?
- What is emerging in your spiritual journey?

The ultimate goal of the spiritual journey is to know our authentic self and our relationship to the sacred. Spirituality includes feelings, thoughts, experiences, and behaviors that arise from a search for that which is generally considered sacred or holy. Transformation is our heritage. Engagement is the key to transformation. You must embrace your reality in order to transform it.

Surrendering and Reclaiming

Patterns and cycles are part of our spiritual journey. Our understanding deepens as we begin to see our part in the patterns. Patterns include finding and losing, surrendering and reclaiming, and enjoying and detaching. Since rhythm is the key to balance and belonging, being in rhythm with your soul empowers you.

In my experience, the journey invites us to claim each aspect of ourselves—surrender and then reclaim. For example, at times I understood that I needed to surrender my will and trust that I would grow and be safe. Other times I called on my will to motivate me to be strong in the face of difficulties or despair. Engaged spirituality is a dance of awakening and surrendering. Surrender is not passivity. In the West, we are taught and rewarded to seek mastery, not surrender. Marianne Williamson, author of *A Return to Love,* offers us her perspective on surrender: "To relax, to feel the love in your heart and keep to that as your focus in every situation, that's the meaning of spiritual surrender."

Discernment is necessary in order to choose which aspect best serves our spiritual quest at any moment. For example, if I had surrendered self-determination while writing this book, you would not be reading it. I surrendered my control when I realized that I had more lessons to learn before I could write the final chapter with integrity. My guides reminded me of the relationship between surrender and trust during a channeling session:

Rosie: Is trusting the same as surrender?

Guides: It depends. At times you are invited to trust that all is in alignment with your highest good. If you are convinced that you know what is best, then surrender is in line. Letting go of a preferred outcome is a form of surrender.

Rosie: At times I have prided myself on my will, which I now appreciate was the opposite of trusting, certainly of surrender.

Guides: As you learn to attune to higher will and then universal will, letting go is easier. Breathe. Be easy. Understand that growth and evolution are incremental. Cooperation accelerates the process. In time (laugh) the choice for the transcendent unity becomes habitual because it delights and unifies all.

Rosie: I deeply desire to live my life from that perspective. I yearn to merge with the transcendent, not as a getaway from ordinary reality, but as a soul seeking unity.

Guides: Once you have been swept into the dynamics of grace, bliss beckons. This is the way of the mystic. Nothing else satisfies. Please appreciate that trust and surrender empower.

Spiritual maturity is grounded in the readiness to let everything go. One of the important lessons in this School of Love is to be able to sacrifice who you are for who you could become. Ram Dass, in his most recent book, *Be Love Now*, challenges us to embody both surrender and contentment. Identifying what creates a sense of inner contentment opens the door to self-love.

The spiritual journey is filled with challenges, paradoxes, and surprises. Spiritual growth has no boundaries but keeps emerging. Learn to risk being in a place where you are more interested in what you don't know than what you already know. Make inquiry a spiritual practice. To the degree that I am invested in seeing things in one way, I limit information from influencing my reality. Grasping for certainty in an uncertain world causes suffering. I felt a renewed sense of creative freedom when I adopted Craig Hamilton's practice of affirming, "I don't know and I want to know." Intuitively, I know that the unknown is the place of discovery and power. When I trust myself to love deeply, I enjoy not knowing so that evolution can break through. I keep a copy of the koan, "The unanswered questions of our lives are our greatest teachers," on my bathroom mirror.

Ego as Trickster Teacher

We do not progress in this School of Love until we know who is in control of our life and why. One way of determining our motivation is to inquire whether our intention is grounded in love, which is aligned with our soul, or in control, revenge, or fear, which are aligned with our ego. One of the assignments of soul is to challenge and transform the ego. Once we make a commitment to aligning with our soul's path, our ego will challenge us. Think of ego as our younger lost and wounded self that controls our behavior until we align our actions with our soul potential. We can count on our ego to try to sabotage our movement toward our authentic self.

The key to letting go of our attachment to ego is to become intimate with its limiting and controlling strategies. Common aspects of ego include:

- Actions driven by fear
- Self-importance
- Arrogance
- Self-doubt
- Being judgmental
- Defensiveness
- Hatred
- Being limiting and contractive
- Self-destructiveness

Our ego is an insatiable and accomplished shape-shifter that can show up in our lives as self-importance one moment and doubt and victim-consciousness the next. According to Swami Muktananda, author of *From the Finite to the Infinite*, "The role of the impure ego is to make you believe that what is bad is good and what is good is bad."

Imagine you are affirming courage, which is aligned with your soul. Sooner or later, fear, which is aligned with your ego, will challenge you. I call this interaction the principle of co-arising. Think of fear as a split off aspect of courage that wants to be integrated. Think of the rainbow from which we draw so much inspiration and celebration. It appears when darkness meets light. Fear is a survival instinct, and whenever the ego feels challenged, it will confront us with low frequency negative emotions, including anxiety, anger, jealousy, and suffering. The key is to be radically honest and inquire: Am I identifying with the low energy frequency of drama, which is connected to my ego, or with love, which is connected with the high frequency of my soul?

Dissolving the ego is the work of the soul. Ego fears an encounter with the soul because it does not want to surrender its control. We can transcend our egos by accessing our high hearts and allowing our intuition to provide high-frequency motivation that transcends our egos. Remember that consciousness beyond ego is the authentic self. Part of the spiritual journey requires that we break away from our ego and align with depth. Truth is expansive. Ego is limiting. Enlightenment is consciousness without ego. When we dissolve our egos, God awaits. In order to override our egos, we must become intimate with them.

❖ Please respond to the following open-ended sentences
  • The voice of my ego sounds like_____
  • The voice of my ego feels like_____
  • The voice of my ego expects me to_____
  • The voice of ego challenges_____
  • The voice of ego yearns for_____
  • The voice of ego's connection with the future_____

❖ In order to engage your soul, you must align with its frequency. Please respond to the following open-ended sentences from the center of your high heart:
  • The voice of my soul sounds like_____
  • The voice of my soul feels like_____
  • The voice of my soul expects me to_____
  • The voice of my soul challenges_____
  • The voice of my soul yearns for_____
  • The voice of my soul's connection with the future___

Take a few minutes and record the connections you made, your questions, and anything that you wish to remember.

I am reminded of an Eastern parable:

Someone asks her teacher: "When we reach enlightenment, will we still have to endure feelings of fear, pain, and sorrow?"

The Teacher replied: "When one reaches enlightenment, smoke still rises, but it no longer sticks to the walls."

Benefits of a Spiritual Practice

The discipline of a regular spiritual practice leads to the ripening of one's spirituality. One of the major reasons we need a spiritual practice is to get beyond the ego, the manager of the personality. In addition, daily practice wears away self-concern and self-absorption. The three basic components of a spiritual practice are daily self-reflection on motives and intentions, daily alignment with the sacred, and daily embodiment of your spirituality in attitude and action. I agree with Deena Metzner who writes, "Maintaining spiritual practice is an ordeal like climbing a mountain, and it demands the same of us: commitment, discipline, endurance, focus, and awareness."

Spiritual practices include:
- Prayer
- Yoga
- Sacred dance
- Solitude
- Meditation

The Practice of Meditation

I invite you to consider that the purpose of meditation is inner happiness, inner peace, and inner joy that lead to the unfolding of your authentic inner being. When you are at peace with your inner self, you will be at peace with everyone. Another purpose of meditation is to still the mind and penetrate the heart in order to unfold the inner being of Divinity.

My friend Jan Phillips puts it this way: "There is nothing anyone has to learn in order to go within. It is simply a matter of quieting down, setting aside time, committing to a practice of solitude and silence. There are no rules to follow, no creeds to learn, nothing to memorize. All that is needed is just the willingness to take some time out of every day and look inward to the greatest gold mine of all."

Most meditation techniques begin with paying attention to your breathing. Breath links body and mind together. However, most of us rarely experience our body because we are either attached to the past or preparing for the future. Consciousness is connected to the body through the heart center. Invite your heart—not your ears—to be conscious of each incoming and outgoing breath. Breathe in and out gently so that your breath remains inaudible to your ears and invite your heart to become conscious of your breathing.

Distraction comes from letting the mind wander about. Notice distractions without letting them hook you. Without attention or attachment, thoughts, feelings, and images arise and disappear. Next, say "thank you," to interfering thoughts and move on. In one Buddhist meditation practice, whenever the mind starts to wander, you say "thinking" and come back to following your breath. You can do the same when your mind throws up a roadblock to change. Take note of any excuses, fears, complaints, negative thinking, or worries that are habitual and irrational. Instead of giving them mental attention say "roadblock."

Meditation helps us develop the witness state. Our inner witness simply observes, without reacting to whatever thoughts, feelings, memories, or pictures pass before us. By not attaching meaning to thoughts, we uncover an impersonal observer that observes without reacting. The witness is not attracted to anyone or anything. The key to meditating is noticing your unique mental patterns of distraction.

Thich Nhat Hahn, author of *Being Peace*, describes mindfulness as an experience of "inner sunshine." Mystics of all traditions agree that meditation brings all the sensing, questioning, imagining, analyzing, and evaluating to a halt. In other words, meditation exposes and then quiets the ego. The scientific benefits of meditation include:

- Relaxation
- Improved immune functioning
- Increased brain synchrony
- Less stress on the nervous system
- Improved health and vitality
- Increased positive thoughts and feelings
- Increased serotonin, which helps to regulate mood and sleep

Remember that meditation is your true nature. We meditate not to attain God, but to become more aware that God is already within us. Anthony de Mello, author of *One Minute Wisdom,* suggests putting your thumbs in your ears for a few minutes to listen to the silence beyond the noise. Zen Buddhists believe that if one sits quietly enough, the stone may be heard growing in the side of the cliff. The Bible tells us to "be still and know that I am God." By intentionally inviting stillness, we become receptive to God's wisdom that speaks through our high hearts. Remember that in our School of Love, meditation is listening to God, and prayer is talking to God.

This journal entry explores my relationship with silence:

In silence, there is nothing to do, nobody to take care of or to please. There is no agenda, goal, or expectation. No need to change or make anything different from what it is. Silence has no boundaries, so I have nothing to protect or defend myself against. The only purpose of silence is to experience and deepen my experience of inner silence.

I intentionally leave all expectations at the door as I commit to stilling myself with silence. I also unburden myself of the multiple lists of things accomplished or things to do. Absent too is the need to prove that I am enough by giving too much of myself. Gradually, I unplug myself from all that makes up my familiar world and prepare myself to befriend the unspoken, the yet to be known to me.

Sometimes I distract myself momentarily from the emptiness that silence holds by tracking my inner experiences, cautioning myself to remember fleeting images, key words, and prominent sensations. After a few moments, I overcome my tendency to control and surrender once again to the unknown as well as the unremembered.

I feel deeply nurtured by the spacious quietness that surrounds me. My breathing slows down. I sigh. My body twitches in response. Sometimes I smile as a childhood memory of being punished by solitary confinement surfaces. How I hated being sentenced to silence.

Now as a seasoned adult, I feel a profound sense of relief when I intentionally embrace silence. I feel the depths of silence as well as its lightness. A few times, I have experienced the whimsicalness inherent in silence. Always, I sense a lightness of being, a deep inner satisfaction and gratefulness for saying "yes" to the "stop, look, and listen," signal within my soul.

Silence is my spiritual food. Renewal awaits me within the silence. Without spiritual nourishment, I neglect my inner life and its movement. Each time I intentionally create the time and space to go within, I enjoy this time of holy leisure and remind myself to make another appointment with silence soon.

Meditation as Brain Food

When we meditate, our brains emit different brain waves. We receive information at a deeper level than we do in normal waking consciousness. Scientists in a laboratory outside Raleigh-Durham, N.C. studied the brain waves of a monk meditating on compassion. They reported a dramatic increase in gamma waves in the part of the brain associated with positive emotions while the monk concentrated on maintaining an open heart. After years of devotion and discipline, his brain had transformed into a different instrument—one that hums with compassion.

In meditation we learn to let go of our compulsions to respond in habitual ways. As we intentionally relax and create quiet inner space, rather than identifying with our thoughts and feelings, we discover freedom.

Recently, I escaped to a motel for three days to concentrate on editing this book. When I registered, I told the owner that I did not need room service or any interruptions. On my final day, someone knocked on the door as I was writing. I did not respond in my habitual way by jumping up to answer the door. Instead I detached my thoughts and feelings from the knock and carried on with my editing. Returning to silence felt nourishing.

Meditation is also a way to surrender into your deeper inner knowing.

❖ Try this meditation-revelation technique and see what happens for you.
  - Breathe deeply.
  - Adopt a knowing heart focus.
  - Write on the top of a blank piece of paper: "Thank you for providing clarity about _____." Take a relaxing breath and let your pen or pencil write. Thinking is not allowed. If your writing seems to stall or pause, write "thank you, thank you, thank you," until the flow resumes.

More meditations can be found in the Appendix.

The Power of Not Knowing and Not Naming

Kenosis is the name for a movement from controlling or being controlled to yielding, from attachment to detachment, from mastery to mystery. It means shedding the script "What do I want to do with my life?" to discover "What is life inviting me to become?"

In a letter to his brother dated December 21, 1817, John Keats referred to the state of unknowing as "negative capability." Being in uncertainties, mysteries, and doubts, without an irritable reaching after fact and reason, describes both kenosis and negative capability.

Children specialize in living their lives from the center of "I don't know and I want to know." My Grandson Noah is definitely a teacher for me in this area. Listen in on a few of his five-year-old questions:

"Our soul loves to love, right, Grandmom?"

"Do you think God laughed at himself when he created the first human?"

"Do ants have more than one lifetime?"

"Do you think bumblebees feed their souls as they drink nectar from our flowers?"

Stories as Touchstones

Telling our personal stories is part of engaged spirituality. According to Jan Phillips, author of *Marry Your Muse,* "The greatest gift we have is the gift of our story." We build our lives on the foundations of stories. The more we invest in a story, the more important it becomes to continue investing in that story. Discernment is an essential resource that helps us to determine whether our story encourages us to expand or contract. Remember, the ego delights each time we relate the story, as that keeps us alienated from our all-knowing hearts. Caroline Myss advises people to avoid telling stories about their wounds and names the tendency to attract others by mutual pain "woundology." Being aware of our motivations for telling and re-telling our stories leads to more discernment.

Dr. Jean Houston believes that our way to holiness is by being punched full of holes. In order to discover what is trying to be born from your wound, she advises that it is time to stop telling your small story, the particulars, the details, and tell the larger story. She encourages people to "tell the tale anew, this time with the wounding in the middle of the story."

When my almost fifteen-year-old son Mike was accidentally electrocuted in the nearby schoolyard, I told the story of his death over and over from beginning to end, some times out loud, sometimes only in my mind. Each time I told my story, I felt the emotional impact and re-lived his death. No matter how many times I repeated the details, Mike and I emerged as victims.

When I followed Jean Houston's advice to begin telling my story in the middle, I was able to acknowledge how Mike's death pierced my heart open, and how my spiritual journey began soon after he died. Beginning from the middle of the story transformed my need to see both of us as victims. I began to relate to myself as a seeker and to Mike as "inspirited" rather than "my dead son." Sometimes love insists we die to who we were, so we can explore the unknown and eventually move into our future. Although I have already asked you to reflect on your personal stories in an earlier chapter, I realize the importance of repetition. May Sarton, author of *Journal of Solitude,* wrote, "I have written every poem, every novel for the same purpose—to find out what I think, to know where I stand."

❖ Reflect once again on your personal stories:
- Which of your personal stories anchors you to your contracted ego and to suffering?
- Which of your favorite personal stories aligns you with soul empowerment and expanded consciousness?
- Make a list of the important touchstones on your spiritual journey. Remember to include both people and events. Next to each entry, record the meaning that you created and note how your meaning strengthened an already existing belief.
- Next, check to see if your meanings have changed over time.

Remember the wise words of Isak Dinesen, author of *Out of Africa:* "All suffering is bearable if it is seen as part of a story."

Balance as Teacher

Balance is a key concept in our School of Love, and balance extends to the time we devote to meditation. Each time I do a soul reading, which is like a meditation for me, I devote equal time to my body. I take care of my body by swimming and hiking. Substantial research confirms the mutual benefits derived from cross-training. My swimming enhances my meditation practice, and my meditation practice deepens my swimming. Because grounding myself in the earth is important to both my body and my soul, and I live in Maine where winter lasts for months on end, I have a large ficus tree that lives in a huge pot, and I have been caught standing in the plant pot with bare feet, reveling in being close to the earth and my soul.

Part of our education in the School of Love concerns the crucial interrelationships between body, mind, emotions, and spiritual energies. Spirit, mind, and body all need nourishment and integrity to thrive. Scott and Helen Nearing, co-authors of *Living the Good Life,* were models of balanced living and loving for me, reminding me how to organize my daily life in a way that honored the needs of my body, mind, and spirit. Here's their formula: dedicate four hours a day to working for sustenance, four hours for creative pursuits, and four hours for socializing with friends.

I do my best, considering the daily demands of my life, to treat my body to daily exercise. Since I get bored easily, I walk, swim, and dance. I meditate and read to satisfy my spiritual needs, I stay in touch with friends either by e-mail or phone, and I care for my two grandchildren daily. Volunteering at the local elementary school and adding my time and energy to Sadhana, a spiritual center in South Portland, satisfy my need for community and service.

The Power of Waiting

Waiting patiently in expectation is the foundation of spiritual life. Believe it or not, soul is the patient part of us. However, we must journey inward to connect with soul in order to experience patience. Growth happens in the waiting times. We need to practice being silent and heart-centered in order to connect with multidimensional knowing. I have trained myself to wait in inner emptiness and fullness of outer expectation. Whenever I am at my impatient worst, I remind myself that someone has to water bamboo seeds for at least six years before the green shoots appear above ground.

I keep this poem in each of my journals to remind me of the power as well as the paradox of claiming stillness:

The seed of mystery lies in muddy water.
How can I perceive the mystery?
Water becomes clear though stillness.
How can I become still?
By flowing with the stream.
- Lao Tzo

The Journey to Inclusiveness

My journey has taken me inward and downward into the depths of pain, grief, longing, and depression, as well as upward and outward towards expansion, luminosity, forgiveness, and healing. Each experience that I attracted added to my spiritual path. One of the lessons of the spiritual journey is to understand and appreciate that every single person who shows up in our life brings a gift. Even darkness carries a gift, if we claim it. Wholeness is our destination. One of my favorite ways of challenging myself is to ask, "In what ways does this person add to my wholeness?" Then I add another challenge by finding at least one reason to be grateful for every person who has entered my life, no matter how briefly. I admit at times this is a difficult question to answer, especially if I am projecting some of my shadow aspects onto my designated teacher. Sometimes a person shows up who has accepted the role of being a shadow wisdom teacher for me. He/she points out what I value by expressing and living the opposite values until I wake up and accept the gift of reclaiming my own values. Richard Bach, author of *Illusions,* says it best:

Every person,
All the events of your life
Are there because you have drawn them there.
What you choose
To do with them is
Up to you.

I remember a quotation by Zalam Schachter Shalom that I recorded in my journal: "One of the paradoxes of spiritual growth is that our challenges are the perfect place to discover love and wisdom. Wisdom comes from all the mistakes we have made."

Recently, I heard myself remind a friend who had judged herself for falling off her path, "It's all your path, and every bit of life is your path. There are no exceptions. The inertia, the darkness, the uncertainty as well as the epiphanies, the shadow wisdom teachers, the deaths and denials are all the path. We have all come here for learning. To our soul, it is all information and learning. Spiritual growth can happen anywhere, any time, with anyone, when we honestly reflect on the deeper meaning of our experiences. There is no such thing as being off the path, for we are the paths."

Stepping back helps us to observe ourselves, especially when we remain engaged in a disagreement way beyond the possible resolution stage. Deadlock lowers your energy. Replaying the scene adds to the downward spiral of negative feelings. In order to recover a position of neutrality, take a breath and ask, "What's good about it?" Do this for at least three minutes.

Sue Monk Kidd, author of *When the Heart Waits,* writes "When we give ourselves to spiritual journeying, we realize God always invites us beyond where we are." The invitation can come in the early morning hours. Listen to how I was called.

The first week of living in the small village of Arroyo Seco, atop El Salto Mountain, about ten miles outside of Taos, New Mexico, was an adventure. At 5 a.m. the ear-piercing sounds of a howling dog, followed by loud knocks on the downstairs door, awakened my daughter and me.

I rolled over onto my side, moaned, and covered my head with a pillow. I hoped the loud yells and knocks were left over from a bad dream. However, the unsettling sounds continued.

I did not know what to do. My daughter and I lived alone, and our closest neighbors, whom we had not met, lived about a mile away.

"New land, new life, and new rules," I said out loud to comfort myself. I walked haltingly downstairs, hoping that if I hesitated, the noise would end.

The outside door was made of wood and had no glass to give a view outside. The howling continued only louder than before. Clutching the top of my pajamas around my throat, I opened the door.

Four Native American men looked me over. A big, gray dog howled. Its back leg was bloody and looked like it had been almost gnawed off.

"How can I help you?" I asked the men.

"This dog got caught in a bear trap. We need your help."

"Who owns the dog?" I asked, stalling for time.

"Mine," each man said, pointing to himself.

"I'm sorry, I said, "I think you have the wrong house. I am not a veterinarian."

"He don't need a doctor. He needs a healer, and we know you are one."

I stepped back. I counsel and guide people and talk to spirits, but I have never called or thought of myself as a healer. Even when I participate in healing circles, I never referred to myself as a healer.

"Look, lady, don't you know there is no difference between a healer of human spirits and a healer of animal spirits? This dog don't have long in this world if we don't do something. Chattering is not healing."

I agreed. "Let's get started," I said with more force than I felt. "Let's do a healing circle and remember this dog when he was healthy and rambunctious. Let's open our hearts and connect with The Great Mystery and send healing energy to the spirit of this dog."

We stood together breathing and sending energy to the dog whose name I did not know. My eyes were closed and I prayed silently for the dog to use our healing energy in the best way. Just before I opened my eyes, I realized that the men who stood on either side of me were holding my hands. To my surprise, the dog was quiet and the bleeding had stopped. The man closest to me opened his arms and hugged me.

"We'll be back again," said the oldest man. "This is a healing place."

I believe the evolutionary impulse of the emerging universe constantly looks for volunteers. Sometimes we consciously know when we have volunteered for service. Other times we seem to stumble into our destiny.

Awakening Your Authentic Power

Authentic self is the creative impulse experience without the limitations of the ego's voice of fear, self-doubt, and self-hatred.

Rumi, the poet who spans centuries, invites us to experience authentic presence:

You were born with potential.
You were born with goodness and trust.
You were born with ideals and dreams.
You were born with greatness.
You were born with wings.
You were not meant for crawling, so don't.
You have wings,
Learn to use them and fly.

The journey beyond ego to authentic self requires deep questioning, internal shifts, giving up the known and often the images of who we think we are. The authentic self seeks depth. Accessing deeper dimensions of self is ongoing, like infinity. When your transformed self breaks through, expect delight, radiance, and inspiration. Marilyn Mandala Schlitz, author of *Consciousness and Healing,* reminds us, "Your behavior, attitudes, and ways of being in the world are changed in life affirming and lasting ways only when your consciousness transforms, and you commit to living deeply into that transformation."

Carolyn Myss, author of *Sacred Contracts,* writes, "Gaining and sustaining authentic power requires dedication, focus, courage, and at times even sacrifice." I have adopted the following definition of power: the ability from within to love, to do, to say, to make, to act, to imagine, to dream, and to make our dreams real.

The power of love is the root of all human experience. Our attitudes and beliefs are extensions of how we love or do not love. The more we grow in personal power and align ourselves with authentic power, the more strongly our loving consciousness impacts everyone around us. We know on an emotional and intuitive level when we are in the presence of a loving person, just as we know when we are around someone with a powerful ego. As long as we reside in our high heart and our authentic power, our ability to discern between people who are embodying love and people who are abusing love feels like a second skin.

The Challenge of Breakthroughs

Consider a breakthrough a move toward your own future and a place where you access even more of your divine potential. What happens after a blast from the infinite? This is the time of ending the trance of your past and daring to explore the edges of your universe. Expect the pull of the past to be present after your epiphany. People who love you will continue to expect you to be available for them in the old familiar ways. Others may intuitively realize that you are different, and although they may be intrigued, they also may be frightened or resentful. Making an intention to continue to expand your spiritual growth is essential.

Yes, there is deep truth in the response to the question, "What do you do after a transformation has occurred?" You "chop wood and carry water." However, once you have made a breakthrough, you have a responsibility to your expanding consciousness to continue to create further evolutionary opportunities. For instance, if you were blessed by creative breakthrough, you have a responsibility to continue creating. If you were blessed with a breakthrough in your thinking, you have a responsibility to continue to keep your mind open and receptive for more epiphanies. Remember that you are a vessel for evolutionary consciousness, and the universe loves a volunteer! Your ability to continue catching inspiration will be compromised if you act as though the Divine has not seized you.

The Spiritual Crises

In the Buddhist tradition, difficulties are considered to be so important to a life of growth and peace that a Tibetan prayer actually asks for them: "Grant that I may be given appropriate difficulties and sufferings on this journey so that my heart may be truly awakened and my practice of liberation and universal compassion may be truly fulfilled."

To become who we are meant to be requires the courage to leave the hiding places of self-protection and to stand at the crossroads of decision. According to Alan Jones, author *of Soul Making: The Desert Way of Spirituality*, the three forms of crises are:

- The crisis of meaning: what should I do with my life?
- The crisis of betrayal by self, others, and life
- The crisis of emptiness or absence

The following condensed version of a recent crisis tells the story of an event that propelled me into a downward spiral, a dark night of the soul.

I had sat with my grandfather Bomp and my Uncle Bud as they were dying. Drawing on my years as a therapist and meditator, I supported them during their dying processes. However, when my dad's dying time came, nothing I knew helped him to let go. I watched, helpless, as he lay in a coma for five days. I was stripped of my belief that I could be a midwife to him as he died. I, who had studied healing for decades, even lifetimes, was unable to help my own father in his journey. I felt ashamed, and it took me weeks to even consider that my presence mattered during his dying.

I wanted him to be easy with himself, to let go, to relax and continue his journey without his debilitated body. He hung on to life, although there was no chance for him to return to the life he had enjoyed with family. He had told each of us he would never end his life in a nursing home. As a result of being with him in his final days, I recommitted to a daily meditation practice as a way to learn surrender, so that when I faced my own dying, I would be able to use my breath and intention to let go of my life.

A liminal crisis is an invitation to cross a threshold between the usual way of understanding ourselves and a new way of being. It is always betwixt and between. The transition demands we leave something of ourselves behind as well as claim a new way of being. Grief makes demands. It requires us to feel and be present for our conflicting and overwhelming emotions. Grief is cumulative. One death reminds us of all the deaths we have survived.

As we surrender to the liminal crisis, we are stripped of our roles, goals, and contexts. Often unexpected change, such as sickness, the loss of a job, the death of a loved one, a spiritual or healing crisis, or depression can activate a sense of insecurity when all that is known dissolves. The inner journey downward is surrounded by isolation, exhaustion, pain, and sometimes depression. I came down with double pneumonia shortly after my dad's death. Isolation and vulnerability accompanied me in my descent into the liminal world.

My friend, Leslie Rosenberg, offered these encouraging words:

Head warns
Beware
Stop
At least take care
Heart and soul know
Push beyond
Believe
The gift awaits.

The process demands that you give up control of the timing, the unfolding, and who you will be when you emerge. Why? If we work our way through our feelings of pride, anger, jealousy, and despair, the gift is our rediscovery of self. The goal is the healing of our emotions through rest, retreat, and self-contemplation. If you accept that life moves us toward our own perfection, it is vital to align with the truth of what life is presenting to us moment to moment. Peter Caddy, co-founder of Findhorn, said that one of the most transforming things you can do to change your reality is to love who you are with, what you are doing, and where you are. Try it!

Bob Monroe, a seasoned seeker, friend, and author of *Ultimate Journey*, writes, "At a particular moment, we reach a point where increased vulnerability meets with deepened awareness. Some decisive remembered event that rearranges our normal perceptions and patterns, enabling newness to break in."

The transformation of self-concept is the work as well as the goal during a liminal crisis. During the transition phase, liminal people envision themselves as they might become. It takes time, motivation, creativity, and optimism. The abiding questions include:

- What did you lose?
- What did you gain?
- What did you re-claim?

If you take advantage of a crisis, or soul initiation, you create an opportunity to merge with a deeper connection to self-love and your soul.

Multidimensional Soul as Teacher

The soul walks not upon a line
Neither does it grow like a reed.
The soul unfolds itself, like a lotus
Of countless pearls.
- Kahlil Gibran

I love the distinction that Nikkos Kazantzakis, author of *Zorba the Greek,* makes between the three kinds of souls and three kinds of prayers:

"I am a bow in your hands—draw me lest I rot."
"Do not overdraw me, I shall break."
"Overdraw me and who cares if I break."

When we align with our soul, we are blessed with a multidimensional way of knowing that is very different from our ego's attachment to analyzing, thinking, and conceptualizing. "You cannot connect to your soul with your mind, you must use your heart," Thomas Moore, writes in *Care of the Soul.* To the soul, memory is more important than planning, art more compelling than reason, and love more compelling than understanding.

Soul-generated thinking arises from an infinite field of knowing that is interconnected to all that is. It is breakthrough thinking where we are connected to intuition, synchronicity, new insights, and the recognition of unseen resources. Direct experience is the province of the soul and gains the attention of the heart. Listen to the heart-centered words of Hildegard of Bingen, an abbess and mystic, born in 1098:

"The visions which I saw I did not perceive in dreams, or sleep, or delirium, or with bodily eyes and the external human ears, or in remote places. I received them while I was awake and of a clear mind, with the eyes and ears of the inner self, in open places, according to the will of God."

Compare her vision to the direct experience of The Christian contemplative, Thomas Merton, author of *New Seeds of Contemplation*:

"Then it was as if I suddenly saw the secret beauty of their hearts. The nether depths where neither sin nor desire can reach, the person that each one is in God's eyes. If only they could see themselves as they really are. If only we could see each other that way there would be no reason for war, for hatred, for cruelty…we would fall down and worship one another."

I know something of what they experienced.

A few months after my third eye energy chakra opened, I was walking on the beach, something I do often, but this time I felt myself connecting with the soul of each person I passed. I beheld each one as a miracle. No exceptions! I even connected with two dogs as souls! Love and delight danced within me in response.

Think of presence as the soul texture of a person. When and where do you feel present in your life? When we align with our soul, our life takes on a new depth and delight. Grounding in soul frequency enables the capacity for joy and spaciousness to deepen. Joy extends to being in the body. Each day is welcomed with expectation and delight.

The Spiritual Shorthand of Soul

Your soul communicates by a different kind of logic. It presents images that are not immediately intelligible, offers feeling impressions, and persuades more with desire than with reasonableness. Metaphor is the literal language of the soul. We go back to the mystics to learn more about the language of soul.

Open your knowing heart to the words of Meister Eckhart, a thirteenth century philosopher and mystic, who describes it this way: "When the soul wants to have an experience of something, she throws an image of the experience ahead of her and then enters into it. It's how we create our lives. We imagine what we want. We get an image of it, speak of it, feel it in our heart, and eventually enter into it."

Open your soul to Hildegard's poem:

The soul is like a wind that waves over herbs,
Is like the dew that moistens the grass
Is like the rain soaked air that lets things grow.
Be a wind, helping those in need.
Be dew, consoling the abandoned.
Be the rain soaked air, giving heart to the weary,
Filling their hunger with instruction
By giving them your soul.

Soul Purpose as Inner Compass

John O' Donahue, author of *Beauty: Rediscovering the True Sources of Compassion, Serenity, and Hope*, reminds us, "Your soul knows the geography of your destiny." When we align with our soul purpose, its frequency entrains our mind, our heart, and our cells

Think about soul purpose as the localized impulse of evolution within us. When we align ourselves with our soul purpose, we resonate with power from our essence self and our capacity to attract and transmit love expands. Imagine that before we were born, we, in collaboration with our souls, designed our unique cosmic report card. Together, we declared our soul purpose, sometimes called a destiny path or mission. Together, we identified specific life lessons or learning experiences in this School of Love. Together, we also claimed specific soul qualities that connect to our healing and power this lifetime.

Think of your cosmic report card as another name for your unique light frequency. The more you align with your soul purpose, the lighter you become and the more love you experience and express. Perhaps that is precisely what Rainer Maria Rilke referred to when he wrote:

"I want to unfold. I don't want to stay folded anywhere because where I am folded, there I am untrue."

Benefits for knowing your soul purpose include:
- Consolidation of energy: You avoid going in inappropriate directions
- Expression of your unique form of creativity which brings about personal and collective healing
- Expansion of happiness, fulfillment, and joy
- Commitment to altruistic service

Your soul's destiny call does not necessarily take you in the direction your ego wishes to go. Yet the truth and wisdom that reside in your soul are irresistible. Your destiny call always takes you in the direction of self-evolution and empowerment. The inner knowing of "I must" signals a destiny challenge. For example, my soul issued a "you must" invitation when I moved from Maine to Taos, New Mexico, during the summer of my daughter's senior year in high school. We left family and friends and settled into a culture and small town where we knew nobody. While living in northern New Mexico for five years, I learned to relate and listen to the earth as Mama Earth and participated in sacred earth honoring rituals. My daughter met and married the father of my two grandchildren. Through the years, I have learned to take action on the first evidence of a soul call because I do not wish to create drama and unnecessary suffering for myself or people I love if I deny or fail to take action once I recognize a soul call.

❖ Here is your opportunity to gain more awareness about your soul's call.

- Take a few gentle breaths and move into your high heart and connect with your soul. Then write whatever comes to you.
- I am here on this earth to_____.
- If I were permitted to bring five memories from this lifetime with me into my afterlife, which five memories would I choose and why?
- What is my unique giveaway to this planet?
- If I had a million dollars and believed I could not fail, what would I do with my life's energy?

Remember our deepest calling is to grow into our authentic selfhood, whether or not it conforms to our inner image of who we think we ought to be. Others should know your vision of the world by how you live, not by what you say. Arjuna Ardagh, author of *Awakening into Oneness,* suggests that you ask yourself if the way you live, day by day, reflects your vision of the world.

Soul Purpose as Teacher

Our soul purpose evolves as our consciousness expands. Souls delight in surprise and your destiny call might surprise you. When I turned 60 years old, after years of teaching, counseling, writing, and sculpting, I said "yes" to a new calling. I made a commitment to live with my daughter and to help her raise her two children, Noah, who is six and Malia, who is now nine years old. Although I was still being of service, my energy was now devoted to loving service to my family. In order to align more deeply with your soul purpose, breathe into your high heart and surround yourself with love.

Remember that when we say "yes" to our calling, we are most vulnerable to our inner critic. Sabotaging ego voices coexist with soul aspects. The principle of co-arising requires us to be alert.

Once you are aligned with your soul, knowledge and wisdom come to you spontaneously. Our own experience is often our proof when we commit to our spiritual journey.

For years, I routinely asked to be used as a resource for the Source each time I did a soul reading. My prayer became "use me, use me, use me." However, I never realized that I did not use the word "God," although I considered God as another name for Source. In November, 2010, I listened to a women relate her experience following the death of her husband who was a minister. She realized soon after his death she had lost not only her partner but also her direction. Depression claimed her. One morning she awoke and knew she needed to turn her life over to God. She did. A few hours later her phone rang, and someone offered her an opportunity to consult with a fledgling community service project.

As I drove home from the meeting, I acknowledged that I had not ever thought of turning my life over to God. Being a strong Maine woman from a lineage of five generations of independent women, I prided myself on being in control of my life. Before I drove the five miles to my home, I made a commitment to invite God in to command my life. Before I went to bed I surrendered my life to God and felt a sense of empowerment and love that continues to bring tears to my eyes.

Be on the look out for the spontaneous outpouring of tears. Tears signal appreciation for the sacred, which is unfolding and evolving. Alan Jones wrote, "Something positive is released when tears flow. Weeping has a triple function. It softens a hardened heart and dries out soul, making it receptive and alive. It clears the mind. It opens the heart."

A question I challenge myself to answer randomly is: What do I know most deeply at this moment? My answer is: I know at the depth of my being that love asks me to go beyond where I am familiar and to explore what is unknown to me yet never beyond me. I know loving is my path and my partner in evolution. I know I will not leave this body and planet until I have learned the lessons of love by loving myself, others, and life herself.

Synchronicity

Ram Dass describes synchronicity as "a wake up call—a signal that everything is inextricably connected in the One." Being aware and attentive to "happenstance" life events is another lesson of engaged spirituality. Synchronistic events are like mirrors, reflecting back to us something of ourselves. They hold the promise that if we will change within, the patterns of our outer life will change also. Consider that synchronicity is at work in our lives when we feel connected, rather than isolated and estranged from others; when we feel ourselves part of a divine, dynamic, interrelated universe.

Each time I spot synchronicity in my life, I experience a deep connection to All That Is, and then I erupt in laughter. Here are a few examples of synchronicity at play in my life:

I was frustrated because I could not figure out how to end the chapter on love. I giggled when I spied a bumper sticker tacked on to a car parked next to mine that read, "When the power of love overcomes the love of power, then we will have peace." For sure, the shift from power to love opens the heart.

Another example of synchronicity happened with the librarians in Scarborough, Maine, where I took up residency to write most of this book. Every couple of weeks, I received an e-mail which informed me that a book I had ordered had arrived. I was mystified because I could not find the title in my file of ordered books. The first time this happened, I wrote it off as a mistake, but nevertheless I checked out the book. The mystery book always arrived at a perfect time and presented me with a necessary insight. About the fifth time I received a pickup notice for a book I had not ordered, one of the librarians confided that she had ordered the books "to help you along."

A commitment to align your life with your soul purpose will transform you and perhaps others. As our hearts and minds expand, we access more and more multidimensional experiences that lead to wisdom. The more we empower our souls, the stronger others feel our Presence. Anodea Judith wrote, "Each person that wakes up to their purpose in the larger scheme of things vibrates with an intensity that is inspirational to others. These actions reverberate throughout the web of eternity, through our relations, into the collective." The truth and wisdom that resides in our souls is irresistible. You will be pleased to discover that you do not have to work as hard to solve persistent problems. Your trance has ended.

Reflective Spirituality Questions

- What delights your soul?
- What risks have you taken on behalf of your soul?
- How would you like to be remembered when you die?
- What are your strategies for maintaining inner peace in a challenging situation?
- What are your spiritual goals and priorities for the next year?
- In what ways, if any, do you sabotage your spiritual commitment?
- How would your life be different if you believed your enlightenment were guaranteed?
- In what ways would your life be different if you imagined you soul's mission was joy?
- Where is home for your soul?
- Who are the intimate friends of your soul?

Awakening Reflective Responses

I invite you to reflect on the Spirituality chapter and record your insights for this day.

- ❖ I Learned_____
- ❖ I Relearned_____
- ❖ I Discovered_____
- ❖ I Rediscovered_____
- ❖ I Regret_____
- ❖ I Appreciate_____
- ❖ Right Now I Feel_____
- ❖ And I Will_____

Journaling Prompts

Here are a few prompts to give you more to wrap your all-knowing heart around. Feel free to agree, disagree, make your own connections, or write your own quotations.

"The new meaning for spirituality is creativity and mysticism." Dr. Otto Rank

"Let your human historical heart merge with your quantum mind so that your deeper calling can be made manifest in space and time." Dr. Jean Houston

"The spirit is that which pressures us from within to evolve." Karl Rahner

"The more you identify with Spirit, the less fear you have of dying." Rosalie Deer Heart

Radical honesty is essential for making the transition into authentic empowerment and claiming your divine legacy. Courage and community are also necessary support for your spiritual unfolding. Why? Our individuality flowers in a community that nourishes the heart, soul, mind and body of all members. Courage and motivation coexist in our consciousness, and in order to grow past the ego, the center of all our learned limited beliefs, we must gain the attention of our soul. To the degree that we are aware of the frequency of our soul, listen, take action, and express gratitude, soul momentum grows.

In my experience, spirituality spills over into creativity and creativity spills over into spirituality. Most of the time I am convinced they are two names for the same process. The key is being heart-centered. When I am centered in my heart, my soul awaits. Creativity, for me, is the outpouring of soul and reverence. Read on to find out how your spiritual journey empowers your creativity.

Creativity

Chapter Seven

Creativity

"Human beings are essentially here for two purposes: to learn to express love and create."
- Angles Arrien

Awakening Creativity

When I approached the blank page to begin writing this chapter about creativity, I tried hard to separate my creative process from my intuition and my spiritual journey. It did not work. For decades, I have related to my three loves as "the three sisters." No matter which one I focused on, the remaining two sisters would always show up. Sometimes they would arrive together. Other times one would visit and make room for the missing sisters. Each added to my discovery or deepening process.

As I look back over three decades, I know that I consciously chose to pursue my creativity. However, it is equally true that there were times when creativity chose me. This reminds me of the latest research on cross-training. Basically, the study says that if you are committed to a spiritual practice like meditation, for example, and you are also committed to a physical activity like swimming or weight training, each practice reinforces the other.

I shake my head and smile because the cross-training research confirms my experience about the dance of creativity, spirituality, and intuition in my life. Here's a journal entry from 1998 about appreciating the intricate interweaving of creativity, intuition, and spirituality.

The similarities between sculpting and soul-making fascinate me. Both sculpting and soul-making embody intention, surrender, risk, patience, and gratitude.

Mary, my friend and sculpting teacher, often reminds me that each stone goes through an ugly state, and my challenge is to continue to be patient and loving. I am reminded that I too go through ugly stages in my spiritual journey when I resist, judge, deny, and allow my ego to believe I am in control of the process.

As I continue to file the stone, I remind myself that I am engaged in a creative process. I understand that I must trust and leave lots of space for wonder and the unknown to surface. Working with the stone helps me to reflect on how I approach other relationships in my life as I wonder what this stone wishes to become. I hold the stone and examine it from all sides. I look for a plane or curve or an interesting texture as a starting point. I invite my imagination in by asking what song this stone might enjoy. Supported by my imagination, I ask inwardly what symbol might emerge if this stone told its story:

File and search.

File and brush off stone dust.

File and listen.

File and trust.

File and pray.

File and connect with spirit of the stone.

File and laugh at myself for trying to force meaning.

File and surrender.

File and breathe.

Then I remember to be curious and imagine this is the first rock I have ever seen. I behold the rock and the beauty I hold in my hands. Then I relax and I imagine that God holds our destiny patiently waiting for us to chisel, file, and sand away whatever stands in the way of each of us claiming our beauty and our destiny. I laugh as I imagine God waiting patiently as each of us questions, seeks, and eventually merges with our essence. Sculpting reminds me that life is a co-creative partnership and everything has a spirit—even a rock!

I agree wholeheartedly with Dr. Carl Jung who said, "The creative mind plays with objects it loves."

Like the spiritual journey, stillness and solitude are prerequisites for creativity. Several times while writing this book I checked out of the home

I share with my daughter and grandchildren and checked into a local motel for a few days. The first time I ran away from home, I felt a bit guilty and made a sign for myself that said, "A Heroine in the Making Creates Here." The emptiness of silence filled me up, and I felt my mind engage with my heart. My imagination scampered as I settled into uninterrupted silence. Once again, I appreciated how creativity flows when I am centered within. During those enriching moments I cannot tell the difference between creativity and meditation. Listen to the wise words of my Dearly Beloved as she gives me a brush-up class on creativity:

When you do not feel inspired, do something else that brings you joy. When you are tired, rest. When you feel you *must* write, do the opposite. Your guides cannot work with you when your mind is busy. Being receptive is an art form. Announcing your openness to collaborate is an invitation. Being present to receive inspiration is your part in this collaborative process. You fall into old habits of linearity when you forget that you are writing about the nature of multidimensional realities where success is measured in joy, not accomplishments. Instead, imagine your life is catching up with your thoughts. For your book or your life to have authenticity, you must live it with consciousness. As you make it your intention to access expanded consciousness, you trigger ideas that exist outside of your time and mind frame. There is nothing esoteric about this process; it is pure quantum physics and you are living in the energy field of quantumness! Delight and joy resonate with the energy of ecstasy. Are you ready to experience and embrace ecstasy as a daily occurrence in your physical life?

Years ago I looked forward to my annual trips to Monhegan Island, home of artists, birds, and fairy houses. Each year I stayed at The Trailing Yew and sat down at the community table to eat two meals a day. I retreated to the island for solitude and creative contemplation, and the loud conversations did not serve my body, mind, or soul. So I designed a large button that I wore on my shirt which read: "Nun on Silent Retreat," and most everyone respected my need for quiet.

Creative Thinking

In addition to practicing creativity with my hands and my heart, I also pursued creativity with my mind. I attended the Creative Problem Solving Institute in Buffalo, New York for the first time in 1974. Inspirational leaders in gifted education, business, government, and the arts taught us the Osborn-Parnes six-step creative problem-solving model. I learned to excel at both divergent and convergent thinking. Best yet, I met Bob Eberle, author of *Scamper*, and he volunteered to mentor me. Later we collaborated and wrote *Affective Education Guidebook* and *Affective Direction*. Although creativity felt like it was in my bones, I felt disconnected from my heart and soul.

For more than 20 years, I taught in the advanced program of the Institute, where I was free to develop and facilitate courses that were considered spin-offs from the original creative thinking model. John Hornecker, author of *Quantum Transformation*, and I designed and taught a course called The Spiritual Foundations of Creativity and Planetary and Personal Transformation. I loved co-creating a community where each day we welcomed guides and teachers, connected with our souls, and invited unconditional thinking to open our minds and hearts to our unique forms of creative expression. My heart cheered! The sisters were all together in one place.

This story reminds me of the link between unconditional thinking and creative thinking:

An elderly Chinese woman had two large pots; each hung on the ends of a pole that she carried around her neck. One of the pots had a crack in it, while the other pot was perfect and always delivered a full portion of water. At the end of the long walks from the stream to the house, the cracked pot arrived only half full.

For two years this went on daily, with the woman bringing home only one and a half pots of water. Of course, the perfect pot was proud of its accomplishments. But the cracked pot was ashamed of its imperfection and miserable that it could do only one half of what it was made to do.

After two years of what it perceived to be bitter failure, it spoke to the woman saying, "I am ashamed of myself, because the crack in my side causes water to leak out all the way back to your house."

The old woman smiled. "Did you notice that there are flowers on your side of the path, but none on the other pot's side? That's because I've always known about your crack, so I planted flower seeds on your side of the path, and every day when we walk back, you water them. For two years, I have picked beautiful flowers to decorate the table. Without you being just the way you are, there would not be this beauty to grace my house."

Creativity as Bridge

I am surprised and delighted when I discover others who share a similar perspective about the world. Enjoy listening to the voices of those who also connect creativity to spirituality:

"I used to think creativity was about things—books, paintings, discoveries, inventions. Creativity is about the heart. Now I believe creativity is our life force, our connection to Spirit." Alison Strickland, co-author of *Harvesting Your Journals*.

"Creativity is a way of living, a spirituality, just as compassion is." Matthew Fox, author of *A Spirituality Named Compassion*.

"One of the ways to connect with the greater spirit of the world is through our creativity." Julia Cameron, author of *The Artist's Way*.

The Call of Creativity

This journal entry captures the dance of creativity and spirituality:

I met a quiet, middle-aged woman at a women's gathering this afternoon. She told me that she had recently "graduated" from a residential psychiatric center. While she was away, someone broke into her apartment and ransacked the two rooms. The only things she really missed were her sculpting tools and her stones.

I told her I sculpted in stone too and I, too, would feel grief-stricken if someone robbed me of my files and stones. I asked her for her telephone number and offered to give her my duplicate files, ratchets, chisels and stones.

"For me," she stammered. "But you don't even know me. You don't even know if I am a good sculptor."

"I know that your heart is good and that creativity is one way you nourish yourself, and that is all I need to know. Besides, this is my graduation gift to you."

She hugged me, and when we moved apart, she seemed as excited as my three-year-old granddaughter.

The minute I walked in my door, I sorted through my tools and put some duplicates aside. Next, I looked through several boxes of stones and chose a few that were not my favorites. As I was about to walk out my front door with the graduation basket, I heard a voice saying," What do you think God would choose to give this woman for a graduation gift?"

I stopped. I shook my head, wondering where the voice had come from. What I knew for sure was God would select the favorite stones and the best tools.

I giggled out loud and then unpacked the basket and selected God's bounty.

When I arrived at the woman's address, nobody answered the door. I placed the basket at the front door and returned home. The next day I drove from California to Maine. I never saw the woman again. I never talked to her, either. Whenever I think about her, I imagine her joyfully sculpting treasures with God's chosen tools. And I smile and feel grateful for the voice that reminded me to give from my heart.

Creative Inspiration

The process of quieting and focusing the mind is common to creative perception, intuition, and meditation. When I reside in my knowing heart, I invite inspiration and multidimensional possibilities. I have learned to choose inspiration over motivation when I am in the midst of a creative project. For example, most days while writing this book, I invited my Muse to guide my writing with ease, fun, and grace. Then I surrendered, wiggled my toes, and waited. However, there were some days when I chose motivation over inspiration and ordered myself to produce a specific number of pages or stick to a five-hour writing schedule. Creativity rarely arrives as a result of a demand. Insights appear when the knowing heart is open.

Listen to my Dearly Beloved's wisdom as she offers insight into my creative process:

<u>Dearly Beloved:</u> Time is a gift, not a pressure. Take your time. Honor your process. Honor your timing. Let go of clock time and abide instead in eternal time. When you let go of your linear thinking that dictates that you must write five hours a day to feel satisfaction, connections happen. The fermentation stage is critical, and that demands you let go. Play with ideas, tease the essential principles out of hiding, and intentionally create space for incubation to flower. Inspiration requires inner quiet. No need to rush. Breathe. Relax. There is no need to do everything at once. Each step is part of the creative process. Your ideas and concepts need to

ferment. Your linear mind continues to track time. Remember it is not about being productive as much as embracing creativity and inspiration. The frequencies reflect your present consciousness!

<u>Rosie</u>: Yes, I understand and I appreciate the difference in the frequencies. I will do my best to detach from my habit of equating time spent on writing with productivity.

<u>Dearly Beloved</u>: Many blessings on your creative and inspiring work this day.

<u>Rosie</u>: Thank you!

Itzhak Bentov, author of *Stalking the Wild Pendulum,* pointed out that creative people rely more on intuition than others and says, "Personal truth can not be found in either analytic thinking or intuitive thinking alone. It can only be uncovered in an open inquiry between them."

Creativity and Empowerment

Creativity is a catalyst for my emergent self. Without creativity, there is no empowerment or authenticity for me. As I commit my knowing heart to my unique creative process, facets of my Being that I have not known were even possible pop up for me to embrace and integrate. Mary C. Richards, friend and author of *Centering,* summarizes my experience:

We have to realize that a creative being lives within ourselves
Whether we like it or not
And that we must get out of the way,
For it will give us no peace until we do.

Listen to the voice of my guides as they add the concept of beauty to the topic of creativity: Enjoy. The source of your enjoyment matters not. Enjoyment is like an open door to the infinite where all possibilities are stored. Enjoyment also beckons creativity. Beauty, too, is meant to be enjoyed and honored with all your senses. Beauty inspires hearts to open wide and inspires love.

Gay Hendricks, author of *The Big Leap,* warns us, "When creativity is not flowing through, life drama happens." I agree, drama and its counterpart, depression, hold a low energetic frequency. Creativity, on the other hand embodies a high frequency. Yet, Eric Maisel, author of *The Van Gogh Blues: the Creative Person's Path Through Depression,* asserts that 100%

of self-nominated creative people will experience depression. "In order to live an authentic, meaningful life, which is the principle remedy for depression, you must feel that the plan for your life is meaningful, the work you do is meaningful, and the way you spend your time is meaningful." Far too often creative people equate meaninglessness with lovelessness.

Depression has claimed me more than once on my journey to wholeness. Each time I moved away from my soul, I felt alone and without hope. Self-love existed only in the distant past. When I asked myself what my soul wanted me to release, the response was immediate:

"Surrender your attachments to what you wish to happen, release all your illusions, seek refuge in your soul, commit to loving yourself, and let go of being another's beloved."

Dr. Bill Plotkin, author of *Soul Craft: Crossing into the Mysteries of Nature and Psyche,* writes about the dark night saying, "The greatest gift of the dark will not be what you find there but how the dark changes you. Offer yourself to the dark and ask it to initiate you in whatever ways it will, making yourself a gift to the dark as opposed to merely hoping for a gift from the dark."

It is possible to experience deep sadness and connect with your emergent soul qualities since both coexist. Should you plunge into depression, your return may be connected to remembered radiance. This is the conscious process of reviewing your life with the focus on remembering specific times when you felt the presence of radiance. No matter how far back in your past, remembered radiance connects you to meaning, and creative people are meaning makers.

❖ Now it is your opportunity to engage your all-knowing heart in a reflection activity.

• Open your heart and gently ask: If this dark night never goes away, what is my soul demanding that I release so I may evolve my consciousness?

Eight centuries ago, Rumi wrote, "For one moment, quit being sad."

Alice Walker, author of *The Color Purple*, writes, "It's like in Native American cultures, when you feel sick at heart, sick in soul, you do sand paintings. Or you make a basket. The thing is you are focused on creating something. And while you are doing that, there's a kind of spiritual alchemy that happens and you turn that bad feeling into something that becomes a golden light."

Remember a time when you transformed suffering into creativity or healing.

- Write about your feelings and your decision to take charge of your energy.

Dr. Martin Seligman, founder of Positive Psychology, conducted an experiment with people who considered themselves severely depressed. He asked them to write down three good things they had experienced each day for fifteen days. When the experiment was over, 94% of the participants had a decrease in depression and 92% claimed their happiness increased. More than seven centuries ago, Hafiz wrote of darkness:

I once asked a bird,
How is it you fly in this gravity of darkness?
She responded, "Love lifts me up."

When I take time to be grateful, I feel happier. Even if the only thing I can be grateful for is my breath, that is a beginning. More will unfold. I am appreciative of the quotation from Meister Eckhart, "If the only prayer you ever say is, 'thank you,'" that is enough."

Welcoming all that arises is true of intuition, the spiritual journey, and creativity. The primary question and quest is, what is my truth? In my experience, it is possible to make meaning out of both the light and the dark. In both instances, when you manifest your unique form of creative expression, you open the doorway to your authentic self.

When I am creative, I become a love magnet. Love nurtures creative expression. Creativity is expansive and self-renewing, and it creates a chain reaction of more inspiration and health. My artist friend, Leslie Rosenberg told me, "Once I have my creative idea, there is only pure joy."

Creativity and healing need one another. Disease is often an opportunity to become more conscious of our motivations, our needs, our desires, our dreams, and our creativity. As you'll see in the next chapter, we can use all our inner resources to heal ourselves physically, emotionally, and spiritually.

Reflective Creativity Questions

- What counts for creativity for you?
- What distances you from your creativity?

- In what ways do you inspire yourself when you wish to amplify your creative energies?
- What can you let go of to create more room for your creativity?
- What actions will you take today to support your creativity?

Awakening Reflection Responses

I invite you to reflect on the Creativity chapter and record your insights for this day.

- ❖ I Learned_____
- ❖ I Relearned_____
- ❖ I Discovered_____
- ❖ I Rediscovered_____
- ❖ I Regret_____
- ❖ I Appreciate_____
- ❖ Right Now I Feel_____
- ❖ And I Will_____

Journaling Prompts:

Here are a few prompts to give you more to wrap your all-knowing heart around. Feel free to agree, disagree, make your own connections, or write your own quotations.

> "A musician must make his music, an artist must paint, and a poet must write if he is to ultimately be at peace with himself. What one can be, one must be." Abraham Maslow

> "When we discover our creativity, we begin to attend to the constant emergence of who we are." John O'Donahue

> "To deny imagination is to cut us off from the holy." Lauren Artress

> "When we create, we come into relationship with what is infinite, unconditional, and unchanging." Oriah Mountain Dreamer

Section Four

The Multidimensional Nature of Healing

Healing

Chapter Eight

Healing

> *"Healing does not mean going back to the way things were before. It means allowing what is now to move us closer to God."*
> *- Ram Dass*

Healing as Teacher

Healing is another invitation to open our hearts. Love is the healing power. Reclaiming optimal health is another course in our School of Love. Dr. Bernie Siegel reminds us that people who experience spiritual joy can heal quite unexpectedly. How about thinking of healing as an active, multidimensional process that includes your perceptions, beliefs, values, emotions, motivations, and karmic past lifetimes?

Health embodies the high frequency of wellbeing. Healing is the experience of remembering and identifying with our essence. Think of essence as your sacred individuality. Once we align with our essence, we can connect more deeply with the totality of our genetic blueprints and empower ourselves to restore optimal healing outcomes. I agree with Sanaya Roman who writes, "Healing is an active internal process that includes investigating one's attitudes, memories, beliefs, and karmic past lifetimes with the intention to release all negative patterns that prevent one's full emotional and spiritual recovery." Wholeness is always present in your energy field.

Most people do not go to their physicians for purely physical concerns. Statistically, roughly 85% of the reasons people visit their doctors are mind/body related. Unfortunately, the average doctor, because of time

179

constraints, listens to a patient's story for only 18 seconds before trying to move to a diagnosis.

Indigenous people create healing rituals that are cosmologically based. For instance, the Navaho people include the story of the universe in their healing rituals. Their healing process invites in the elements of water, air, fire, and earth, as well as the spirits of the ancestors. Jeanne Acterberg, author of *Imagery: Healing, Shamanism, and Modern Medicine,* echoes our interconnection to all that is. She writes, "Health is an intuitive perception of the universe and all of its inhabitants as being of one fabric. Health is maintaining communications with animals and plants and minerals and stars. Health is seeking out all of the experiences of creation and turning them over and over, feeling their texture and multiple meanings. Health is expanding beyond one's singular state of consciousness to experience the ripples and waves of the universe."

The Multidimensional Nature of Healing

According to vibrational or energy medicine, when you have an illness, it travels from the spiritual body through the emotional and mental body and into the physical body. The purpose of vibrational medicine is to reunite the personality with the higher self. Vibrational medicine attempts to heal illness by manipulating these subtle energy fields via directing energy into the body instead of manipulating the cells and organs through drugs or surgery. Dr. Norm Shealy, author of *Soul and Medicine,* reminds us that human consciousness reflects the qualities and intentions of our soul consciousness, and physical and psychological illness can result when they are not in alignment. A lesson or meaning is always attached to an illness. Recovering the meaning you attach to your pain or illness is another course in the School of Love.

According to quantum theory, every positive choice coexists with multiple possibilities—some of which are diametrically opposed to the choice. When you trust your body to heal, your choice coexists with choices and memories of former poor health, phobias, fear of death, and optimal health. The principle of attraction applies here. We attract whatever we focus on and identify with. Since healing and disease coexist, we will attract healing potentials if that is our focus. However, if we identify with our disease or pain, we will add energy to our disease. I vividly remember the day I answered the phone and heard a woman say, "This is Irene, the cancer woman." I breathed and said forcibly, "Please do not describe yourself in that way. Cancer is not your identity."

Once we acknowledge that we have all of the inner resources we need to heal ourselves from the inside out, we must take responsibility for weeding out any low frequency energy and limiting beliefs. Dr. Norm Shealy writes, "Our attitudes affect our susceptibility to disease as well as our ability to overcome pain and disease. When we consciously bring our minds and hearts to a similar vibration so they are functioning in the same vibrational range as our soul, there is a resonance between them and reciprocal communication between their energies. This allows healing to flow effortlessly through the body."

The intent of the soul is for our body to be healthy. Intention shapes outcome. It provides the motivation, the power, and the energetic frequency that determines whether the outcome is healing, further debilitation, or death. Our beliefs determine how much healing we receive. Dr. Bruce Lipton, biologist specializing in mind/body medicine and author of *The Biology of Belief* shows how the mind affects body functions. A change in belief has a direct effect on our cells. "When someone has a sudden shift in belief, it can radically change the epigenetics, which means that the same genetic code will now be interpreted completely differently—this could be the difference between cancer and remission."

A Multidimensional Healing Intervention

Open your knowing heart to this unusual multicultural, multidimensional story:

I picked up my phone and heard an unfamiliar voice say,
"Selo's been shot. He won't go to the hospital. Come quickly."
Selo, a Lakota Sioux medicine man and pipe carrier, sat in the corner of a dimly lit room. As I walked closer I smelled the blood even before I saw the deep hole in his upper leg. The combination of heat from the fire and the smell of fresh blood made me nauseous and I held my hand over my mouth.

I asked, "Why did you send for me? How can I help? You need to be in a hospital."

He interrupted me, "Stop talking your nervous white woman's talk and ask my grandmother to tell me when the next UFO will fly over."

I shook my head from side to side, feeling like I had walked into a very bad movie. Then I regained my voice and stammered, "Selo, I have never seen a UFO. What makes you think I have access to their schedules, even if they do have schedules?" As I spoke the words, I was aware that the conversation seemed bizarre. Here I stood, arguing about the existence of UFOs with a man who might be dying.

"Just talk to my ancestors. They will tell you. It was my mother's mother, my grandmother, who told me when I was a little boy that I would be shot in the leg and now it has finally happened. And she told me that the only way my leg would heal was by a UFO. Now her prophecy is part true." He continued. "I am not dying now. Don't worry. Today is not my dying time. But if I am not there when the UFO passes over, I will die before I am ready."

I still felt nauseous and anxious. I did my best to reduce my inner stress response by reminding myself that I had channeled information from the ancestors many times. However, nobody had ever ordered me to get information before.

As if he read my thoughts, Selo, commanded, "Stop fidgeting with your thinking and talk to my Grandmother."

Okay, Selo, I will do my best. What was her name?"

"Grandmother," he replied.

"Of course," I said to myself.

I breathed gently, which was difficult given the combination of the smells of smoke and blood. Eventually, I connected with an energy that felt like "Grandmother" and thanked her in advance for her guidance.

"Tomorrow 3:15," I announced, relieved and happy to have an answer. Immediately, Selo, asked, "What time of day, afternoon or morning?'

Inwardly I asked, and received the energetic impression, "afternoon."

"Can't they get here sooner," snapped Selo. "I am in big pain."

I snapped back, "Selo, I am not in charge of any of this. I can only give you information and pray it is accurate. If I had any influence, I would order a UFO here now."

"Me, too," he said less gruffly. It's in the hands of the Grandmothers, now. Okay, I meet you at the top of your mountain tomorrow by 3:00. Have lots of black coffee ready. Okay?"

"Yes, of course. Just like always," I said, anxious to be on my way.

Most of the rest of that day I worried that my information had not been accurate.

True to his word, Selo arrived close to 3 p.m. with about ten of his friends. They helped him climb the stairs to my outside deck which had a wonderful view of the huge sky. He wore baggy pants, and I was relieved to be unable to see his wound.

Everyone stood around slurping black coffee and scanning the sky. I prayed silently. Around 3:15, Selo erupted with a loud, keening sound and began dancing in small and then wider circles. I saw nothing, felt nothing, and had no idea what was happening. Clearly, Selo was reacting to something. I scanned the faces of the others and nobody showed any emotions. All eyes were on Selo.

His movements ended as abruptly as they began. He looked at us and said, "All healed. It is done. I am peaceful. I waited more than six times ten years for Grandmother's prophesy to come true. No more scare and waiting. It is done just as she said. Time for more black coffee now."

I noticed he no longer needed help coming down the stairs. He seemed more agile.

Both the local police and the tribal police were outside waiting as Selo left. One of them said sarcastically, "All healed, Chief?"

Selo smiled. Then I watched as he unbuckled the silver belt on his jeans and dropped his pants to the ground, and pointed to his right thigh. No bloody, open red flesh. Not even any trace of dried blood. His thigh was normal, as if he had never been shot.

I gasped. How was this possible? I scanned the sky again. Nothing unusual that I could see. I felt filled with unknowing and questions and gratitude.

Then Selo pulled up his pants, buckled his belt, and walked towards me, "Thanks to you and my Grandmother. I don't have to wait any more days to be shot."

I sighed and thought to myself, "Right! And I don't have to know in advance about the flight schedules of UFOs."

Even now when I remember all of the emotions that I experienced in relation to the miracle of Selo's healing encounter with the UFO, I do not know how to put all the pieces together—and I was present. Did his grandmother see through time when she predicted that he would be wounded? What was her connection with the UFOs, or did she even have one? Did Selo's belief in her prophecy have anything to do with his being shot? Did his love for his grandmother act as a placebo to activate his innate healing ability? I cannot answer these questions with my ordinary mind. This whole healing story is grounded in multidimensionality.

The Healing Power of Love

Relationships give meaning to life. The quality of relationships has much more to do with how often we get sick than do germs, environment, and basic physiology. Connection gives us a purpose for living. Meaning and relationships are strands of connectedness. Perhaps that is the underlying reason why Alan Briskin believes that "healing is fundamentally relational."

Research done at the Institute of HeartMath revealed a fascinating phenomenon. This work tended to confirm the theory that love is a real healing energy with measurable physiological effects, even at the DNA level. One experiment involved meditators who were able to produce a coherent love-associated heart pattern. A special coil was hooked up to a tree to create living antennae that would measure the earth's local magnetic field while the meditators generated love-energy. During the moment of love's presence, a coherent series of spectral-frequency harmonics appeared in both the loving meditator and the earth's local magnetic field, as measured by the nearby tree. Measurements were in frequencies up to and including 7.8. megahertz. The implication of a resonant energy connection between loving emotions and the planetary magnetic field are profound.

The Meaning of Illness

Consciousness is the first place to explore when we are in need of healing. Leonard Laskow has outlined levels of inquiry for getting to the source of an illness:

The first level of source of an illness consists of perceptions and interpretations of events, which establish a holographic pattern of beliefs, thoughts, and feelings.

The second level of source of an illness involves love, worthiness, and a sense of value and their polarities. The deeper meaning beneath the core belief "I'm not good enough" is the belief "I'm not good enough to love or be loved." This causes shame or guilt, which leads to the belief "I'm unforgivable" and other forms of victim consciousness.

The third level of source of an illness deals with choice. Along with this may come a sense of our power and freedom to choose, or a sense of our separation and alienation when we don't express a choice.

The fourth level of source of an illness deals with the choice to be separate from or at one with Spirit or God. We are free to become whole and healed to the extent to which we know and relate to something greater than ourselves.

What would happen if you adopted the belief that healing is the act of accepting your own capacity for grace? Remember that sometimes grace manifests as synchronicity, and at other times it lifts us into an altered state of consciousness. Sometimes grace is the energy that suddenly illuminates us with understanding, allowing us to see what we had not been able to grasp before. That's what happened to me as I worked to heal my twice-injured knee.

I knew my injured right knee had an important message for me. Initially, I had dislocated my kneecap. It was painful, and I chose to be immobile for longer than I care to write about instead of agreeing to surgery. Then a few weeks later, I tore two ligaments in the same knee. The pain was even more severe than the first injury. As before, my doctor ordered ice, leg elevation, and a steel reinforced knee brace and, of course, he manipulated the muscles and ligaments.

During my recovery time, I remembered a quotation attributed to Carl Jung, "God is what you stumble over," and questioned what I was missing. I sensed an intuitive message awaited me, except I did not have a clue what it was. However, after four weeks of resting and tending to my two rambunctious grandchildren, I gave myself the gift of a 36-hour getaway retreat. My agenda was resting, reading, sitting in a hot bathtub, and praying.

Driving was painful, and my doctor advised against it. However, I drove to a motel within twenty miles of our house and checked in before 10:30 a.m. The bathtub was outfitted with attachments to help me get in and out. And the woman who checked me in told me to ask the chambermaid for two extra pillows which were locked in the storage cabinet.

The cleaning lady was in the hall and offered to bring me the two extra pillows. When she delivered the pillows a few minutes later, she asked me what happened to my leg. Then she told me she did Reiki healing and offered to give me a treatment. Her name was Rashina, and she was almost the same age as my daughter.

I must have fallen asleep during her healing session, and when I awoke three hours later she was gone. My leg felt light and free of most of the pain. I wrote Rashina a thank you note and enclosed some money to express my gratitude. I remembered nothing about the healing.

Before supper I went to the lobby to leave the note. The woman at the desk looked at me strangely and said, "Nobody by that name works here. Are you sure you got her name right?"

"Yes, she is about 35 years old, dark skin, long black hair," I said as if describing the woman would make her remember.

The owner shook her head and said, "The only chambermaid I employ is a middle aged Scottish woman with short, white hair." End of conversation.

"But what about the two extra pillows that Rashina brought to my room?"

The owner shrugged and half smiled.

This was certainly a mystery, and it didn't end there. During the night I felt gentle pressure, like light vibrations on my right knee. Sort of like a gentle chiropractic adjustment. I could feel my knee pulsating in a pleasant sort of way. I half woke up and heard a voice saying, "You are 80% healed. Be gentle and watch where you are walking, and your knee will be healed ahead of the projected time."

I turned on the light and looked around the room. Nobody was there. Then I smiled because I never measure things in percentages.

Early the next morning I approached a different woman at the front desk. Again I tried to hand Rashina's note to someone. Instead I received the same response, "Never heard of her!"

Still pondering my experience and trying to come up with a logical explanation for the mysterious Rashina, I decided to take a leisurely, hot bath. While bathing I decided that the only explanation that made any sense was that I had been visited by an angel.

The following day, I went for a doctor's appointment.

"You look rested. How are you feeling?" inquired my doctor.

"Great! My knee is 80% healed. I'll bet you will be surprised."

He did not reply but told me to sit on his table while he checked my injured leg for strength and mobility.

He looked puzzled and checked my leg a few extra times. After noting his findings, he said, "Indeed, I agree with you. You are at least 80%

healed. Three days ago I would have put you at about 20% recovered. What happened?"

I had been waiting to tell him.

"Do you believe in angels?" I asked and without waiting for a reply added, "Have you ever been visited by an angel?"

"No, I can't honestly say I've been visited by an angel," he said thoughtfully. "But, yes, I do believe in the presence of angels."

"Well, if you had been visited by one, I think you would know, at least eventually." I told him I knew an angel had visited me.

"Well, I agree something *big* happened to you."

That was enough for me.

The story did not end there. My minister, Reverend Fred Gagnon, dropped by for our weekly visit. I was walking normally and he asked what had happened. How had I recovered so fast?

Without rehearsing my story, I began telling him about my experience at the motel. He listened attentively. Then he surprised me by asking if I would tell the story in church. He had been thinking about doing a hands-on healing ritual in church, and my story would add a personal note. We both agreed we were dancing on the edges of our comfort zones and we both decided to challenge ourselves.

I told my story and felt strong and excited. My cheeks were red and I felt energized. When I returned to my seat, Malia hugged me and squeezed my hand.

As I stood with Fred after the healing service, four people shook my hand and told me in whispered voices that angels had visited them, too, and I was the first person they had told. I left the church wondering how many others had been visited by angels and kept their stories to themselves. Then I wondered what kind of a world we might live in if we intentionally called on angels of healing for assistance.

The Anatomy of Illness

An illness is often a wake-up call from our consciousness calling attention to something. Perhaps we are feeling guilty, fearful, unloved, or any other low frequency emotion. We may be harboring limiting beliefs about ourselves, others, and the world. Expressing gratitude for the wake-up call begins to align our energies with higher frequency possibilities that coexist with the illness.

Some scientists have concluded that 70-80% of all illnesses are largely related to and preceded by the "giving up" syndrome. In other words, the person identifies with the victim archetype. In 1950, internists, psychologists, and psychiatrists at the University of Rochester began conducting studies on what they eventually named the "giving-given up complex." This is the state of mind, generally temporary and related to changes in life circumstances, that was found to be a factor affecting susceptibility to many kinds of illnesses. According to Dr. Bernie Siegal, characteristics include "helplessness, a depreciated image of self, and a loss of gratification from existing relationships or roles in life." See if you identify with any of the following payoffs for having an illness:

- Being a victim—manipulating out of apparent illness
- Being a martyr—suffering in silence to punish another through the use of guilt
- Attention-getting—feeling important because of the attention
- Avoidance—avoiding responsibility for growth

In *Love, Medicine and Miracles,* Bernie Siegel reflects that physical illness "can be a way of gaining love or nurturing. It can become a patient's only way of relating to the world, the only control one has over life." Thus it becomes a treasured wound. He urges us to think of illness as a power disorder, because he believes that disease may serve as a redirection or reset button.

Indicators of susceptibility to disease include:

- Sense of helplessness
- Attitude of giving up
- Loneliness
- Difficulty receiving pleasure
- Inability to ask for and receive care
- Stored anger, fear, guilt, self pity, shame
- Difficulty giving or receiving love
- Avoidance of forgiveness
- Tendency not to trust

Pain and illness often show up as double agents in our School of Love. Instead of adopting an attitude of resignation or dwelling in self-pity, blame, or resentment about an illness, begin to look for specific lessons that you are being challenged to wrap your arms and heart around. Give yourself the freedom to be infinitely curious and kind to yourself as you discover possibilities. By shifting our attention from why is this happening *to* me to why is this happening *for* me, you can connect with the deeper meaning of your illness. The next time you or someone you love has an illness, you may wish to consider the following questions:

- What benefits are you receiving as a result of your illness?
- What does your illness mean to you?
- Who would you be without your illness?

Dr. Candace Pert sees the body as the outward manifestation of the mind and body and brain in combination. In healing any imbalance, one must involve both heart and mind.

Dr. Elmer Green has proven that an enormous surge of electrostatic energy occurs during healing. When we are standing still, our breathing and beating heart will produce electrostatic energy of 10-15 millivolts on the EEG amplifiers. During a healing intervention, Green recorded healers produced voltages of up to 190 volts. Consider this: When we hold a focused healing intention, we may be capable of altering the very molecular structure of what we intend. For instance, be aware of the thoughts and feelings that existed right before you were aware of aligning with low frequency beliefs. I include the following story from my journal to point out how worry can interfere with a high-energy feeling such as optimism and can prevent healing. I learned how powerful my intention was when I finally let go of worry and embraced my healing potential.

I decided to attend a gathering for a young guru from India because one of my friends was his devotee. She quoted him often, and I was impressed with how she had changed since she began studying with him. The auditorium was packed with people of all ages. Most of the adults who wore white clothes were his disciples. I watched as they looked lovingly and longingly at him, as he spoke gigantic truths in simple words. English was his fifth or sixth language, yet I imagined that he would still speak in words of no more than two syllables, even if English were his first language.

When people asked him questions, his favorite answer was "Why not?" I understood early in the evening that anything was possible in his belief system. After the lecture, I was invited to join others for a private reception. Rather than join a large group of people, I felt a need to go outside for some quiet time.

My reflection spot was a small, enclosed meditation garden with a wooden bench. I sat on the warm bench and closed my eyes and tried "just being." Stillness did not come.

A familiar voice asked softly, "Care if I join you?"

My eyes were closed but I recognized the gentle voice of the young guru. "Please do," I said, motioning him to join me on the bench.

"Your mind is overflowing with busyness," he said gently, without a trace of judgment. Then he continued, "Fear is taking up much of the room. Only space for a tiny ray of light."

I sighed deeply. He was right. I had allowed fear to rule my life. I had to move within a week. I had no car, little money, and I had just ended a marriage. I spoke none of my worries out loud.

He continued, "You can let go of the fear if you choose. I can help you. I am here to help you. But if you said goodbye to your fears, who would you be?"

In a moment of truth, I knew he could facilitate a fear release. And he was right; I had no clue who I would be without fear residing in my energy field. I also realized that fear held me back from taking the next step in my spiritual journey.

"It's okay if you are not ready," he said nodding his head. "Perhaps fear is not done being your teacher."

How and where had he learned to make such an astute intervention? As a former therapist, I applauded his wisdom and technique. Another part of me wanted to label him an upstart, which is a word my grandmother might have used!

I started to cry. When I opened my eyes, he was still sitting there, smiling.

"You know," I said very seriously, "I have to participate in this releasing process. I cannot allow you to eat my fear. After all, I created this drama and I need to be responsible for releasing the fear," I said a little too loudly in my best therapist's voice.

"Sure," he said and giggled. "Okay if we begin now?"

"Why not?" I replied and laughed a genuine laugh.

Without further conversation, he began to chant in Hindi. Since I didn't know any words in Hindi, I began to pray out loud. Our voices harmonized and then we both became silent at the same second. Then I felt a mantle of fear lift from my shoulders. I gasped as I felt my heart open. My stomach was next to release old fear. I belched forth old scars. My body began to shake and I could not control the shaking. Finally, laughter exploded from the bottom of my belly.

After who knows how long, he said to me quietly, "You feel *you* now?"

I nodded. I had no words.

"Now it is time to be miracle," he said. "Watch, don't be in your mind."

I watched. He was wearing a long, white sari that touched the ground. His right hand moved slightly and he manifested a rose out of what looked like thin air! He smiled and with a bow, handed me the perfect red rose. It even had thorns on the stem! Still the skeptic, I asked if I could look up his sleeve. I had no idea what I expected to find. Maybe a garden.

He giggled and responded, "Why not?'

His sleeve was not loose enough to hide a rose, to say nothing of a garden. I felt embarrassed and realized I was certainly in my mind, not my heart.

"Now listen, you," he said somewhat sternly. "You, too, can make bouquets happen out of the air. You are a healer. That is why your hands have sweat and feel like white-hot fire. Now that you are without fear, you, too, can create flowers and bouquets and even gardens from the air. The rose you are holding is nothing. Remember miracles are God's way of saying, "Hello."

I closed my eyes in order to remember all that had happened. When I opened my eyes, I was sitting alone on the wooden bench holding the rose that the guru had given me. Beauty had replaced fear, and I sent out gratitude. Then I exploded in giggles.

Strategies to Promote Well-Being and Health

- Tell the truth
- Commit to a spiritual practice and do it consistently
- Resolve emotional conflict
- Adopt a positive attitude
- Savor your positive experiences
- Express gratitude daily
- Be compassionate to yourself and others
- Invest energy and time in your most heart-centered friendships
- Choose curiosity over fear

- Activate and access your intuition
- Laugh
- Dare to give and receive love daily
- Volunteer
- Commit to a physical fitness program
- Believe that anything is possible
- Record your dreams and act on them
- Pray

God as Healer

In a December 12, 2003 poll, Newsweek magazine reported that 77% of Americans believe God can cure people who are given no chance of survival by medical science. Mark Twain had it right when he wrote, "God cures and the doctor sends the bill."

"God is an energy, a healing force that can be experienced within the human psyche, within others and the world at large," wrote Hildegard of Bingen, the twelfth century mystic. She called this healing force *viriditas*, the "greening power of God." Nine centuries later, Mark Matousek, author of *When You are Falling, Dive*, draws our attention back to Hildegard saying, "Every situation has the potential for this greening, this viriditas, this bringing of beauty, insight, or healing from the manure of suffering."

Take a gentle breath and move your energy into your high heart. Surround yourself with love.

- Connect with your guides, teachers, and God and respond to these questions from the fullness of your all-knowing heart:
- If you could ask God five questions about healing, what would you ask?
- How does God experience you?
- How has God, as healer, shown up in your life this week?
- What is your role in assisting God?

Audrey McInnis, a Unity minister and my spiritual mother, reminded me often when I was working through a life challenge, "God is growing you up, Rosie."

Our mental and emotional healing comes from rebalancing our thoughts and feelings to be in touch with our wisdom mind rather than our inner critic. Our physical healing is promoted as we shift our perspective from pain, fear, and loss, to inner strength, joy, and opening to grace.

Our spiritual healing comes from opening our deep heart to love, joy, and meaning, which allows us to love all and serve all.

"Compassion is one of the highest of all energy attractor power patterns," Dr. David Hawkins reminds us. I offer this journal entry that points out the healing power of compassion:

I traveled to Crestone, Colorado from Taos, New Mexico, with two friends to pray at the church dedicated to the Divine Mother. My son, Mike who was electrocuted in the schoolyard when he was 15 years old, would have been a 31-year-old man. On this anniversary of his birth, he had been dead, or "inspirited" as I called it, more years than he had been alive. My body ached. I felt distant from him and his life as my son. Instinctively, I knew that this event was a passage and I did not want to participate.

The church was round and filled with light. I sat in one of the pews and begin to pray and weep. My eyes were closed. An image of a presence appeared as Mary and filled my inner sight. I felt captivated by her energy and wondered why she had joined me. It was her eyes that drew me. She looked at me with deep love and boundless compassion. Suddenly something switched and part of me was behind her eyes gazing at myself! From the perspective of Mary's eyes, I too felt love and compassion for myself as the mother of a dead son.

In a way I still have no adequate words to describe, my grief became filled with light. Grace visited. My tears changed to appreciation for the time Mike and I were together, which was very different from the heavy grief of missing him. I left the church feeling different. Uplifted, and in awe with the understanding that Mary, too, had outlived her son. I said to my friends, "I just received a healing."

I wholeheartedly agree with Dr. Norm Shealy when he says, "Healing mediated by consciousness and activated by intention occurs when the patient's energy system is triggered to conform to the soul's blueprint." Furthermore, I believe that our soul's blueprint is encoded in our DNA. Think of a blueprint as an energy template. Love is the energy that connects you to your entire blueprint archive. I love this quotation from Caroline Myss: "Healing happens when we feel a loving energy flowing freely within us again. Healing is a doorway toward opening the heart."

Listen in on a tutorial from my guides:

<u>Guides</u>: Blueprints are archetypes. Archetypes, by their very nature are multidimensional. Blueprints carry essence, although they provide a form as well. Each blueprint contains and embodies a keynote, and that is important to remember. If we say God is the divine blueprint and one does not believe in the concept of God, the concept of blueprint can be too easily dismissed. If we say blueprints are part of the akashic records and one does not have a clue what the akashic records are, the concept will be disregarded. So let's bow to science and say that a hologram is like a blueprint. Each hologram has a keynote, and all is contained in each of the parts of a hologram. All the elements that make up the wholeness of healing coexist with all the elements that make up disease. Now imagine an electromagnetic energy field surrounding the hologram. We know that energy field as God. Others may be more content imagining it as a force field.

<u>Rosie</u>: Could you please slow down just a bit? Not only am I racing to type your words, my mind is rippling trying to take in all of this information.

<u>Guides</u>: Yes, slow down a bit. Be aware which mind you are engaging: human or quantum. Might you make an energetic adjustment and employ your quantum mind?

<u>Rosie</u>: Yes, please give me some time to frame my intention and let go of my limited thinking. I do appreciate your patience.

<u>Guides</u>: We forget at times that you fall back into a human frequency because we experience you as multidimensional while you are adjusting to expanded ways of knowing your energy.

<u>Rosie</u>: Okay, I will breathe into my high heart and thank my guides in advance for realigning me with the universal mind. Then I will remember that guidance can come and go beyond the speed of light. Next I will smile and remember how much fun this expansion process is for me.

<u>Guides</u>: Happy healing!

The Call to Healing

The holographic principle says that every piece contains the information of the whole. The principle is mirrored in the fact that every cell in the human body contains the master DNA library for how to create an entire human being. The holographic paradigm has implications for so-called hard sciences like biology. Keith Floyd, a psychologist at Virginia Intermont College, pointed out that if the concreteness of reality is but a holographic illusion, it would no longer be true to say that the brain produces consciousness. Rather, it is consciousness that creates the appearance of the brain as well as the body and everything else that we interpret as physical.

Such a turnabout in the way we view biological structures has caused researchers to point out that medicine and our understanding of the healing process could also be transformed by the holographic paradigm. If the apparent physical structure of the body is but a holographic projection of consciousness, it becomes clear that each of us is much more responsible for our health than current medical wisdom allows. What we now view as miraculous remissions of disease may actually be due to changes in consciousness, which in turn effect changes in the hologram of the body. Similarly, controversial new healing techniques such as visualization may work so well because in the holographic domain, thought images are ultimately as real as what we call reality. Even vision and experiences involving non-ordinary reality become explainable under the holographic paradigm.

An Invitation to Holographic Healing

Holographic healing happens from the inside out. You reclaim parts of yourself that you have worked hard to master. Remember that from the multidimensional perspective, time is elastic, and we have all lived many lifetimes. Our pasts belong to us, offering us resources, knowledge, and wisdom. The purpose of accessing our specific blueprint is to promote healing from our lifetime experiences. Each lifetime is a potential resource. Since time is elastic, you may choose to move into your future in order to create and choose an optimal healing blueprint.

Blueprints are energy templates, and each one carries a detailed action plan for optimal wellbeing. Our blueprints are like X-rays that exist in the morphogenetic field as well as in the individual DNA. Think of the blueprint as a computer chip. All the information we need to return to wholeness is encoded on our computer chip.

The downloading process is simple. Once we signal a willingness to remember the existence of our healing blueprints, the energy field opens and expands. Access depends on our willingness to experience and explore our healing resources. Why would anyone hesitate to activate his or her healing potential? Possibilities include: fear, habit, control, a rigid mindset, and perhaps the presence of entities in the field that do not wish to be homeless.

Once we have activated the genetic blueprint, our energy field becomes magnetic. Others will feel the intensification and lightening of our energy field, and they will feel uplifted by our presence. Once the blueprint is reactivated, integrated, and affirmed, the person's perspective becomes one of spaciousness.

Think of healing as a dance of high frequency energies. You empower yourself when you learn how to do this. Here's how.

- Create a focused healing intention by aligning with unconditional loving and unconditional thinking.
- Quiet your mind.
- Affirm that healing is part of your cellular and akashic memory.
- Affirm that your all-knowing heart's intention is to restore wholeness and wellbeing to your body.
- Remember a specific time when you felt healthy, vibrant, and filled with love.
- Release all limiting beliefs.
- Smile and empower yourself by saying a whole hearted "yes" to your magnificence.
- Breathe into your high heart and call in your ancestors. Welcome each one and thank them for witnessing, supporting, and grounding your healing process.
- Focus your magnetic intention on retrieving an optimal healing blueprint from your akashic records. First, check out your optimal health records from past lifetimes.
- Remember that time is elastic and it extends into the past as well as the future. If you choose, gently move into the future, leading with your essence, which is the aspect of yourself that knows how to operate between dimensions.
- Download the optimal health and well being blueprint.
- Make a commitment to repeat a daily healing affirmation for 28 days. The daily affirmation I use is, "Thank you for activating my optimal health blueprint, which resonates in my DNA."
- Move around and congratulate yourself on being a healer.

Here's what a friend of mine wrote after she took my suggestion that she use this strategy to assure she remained healthy after a minor surgery procedure:

"My family stands witness. They circle around me smiling reassuringly. I search for a past lifetime that holds an optimal blueprint, and it doesn't feel right. I look into the future, remembering a story about people learning to balance the energy of their life force to heal themselves, a future where doctors serve as counselors to help people heal themselves without drugs or surgery. I love that possibility, so I choose to claim it as true for myself right now.

I create the image of a woman's body, my body, shimmering with blue light that suggests health and vitality, and call it to myself to merge with my body sitting cross-legged on the bed. As it comes nearer, my body begins to tingle with anticipation. I watch it gently move into the image of my physical body, and my smile widens into a delightful grin. I didn't think I could do it but I did. I look to see if my ancestors, including my brother who died this year, are still surrounding me, and they are smiling. They break into applause. I'm smiling with delight. I open my eyes, get up and look into the mirror. My face looks flushed with pleasure and my eyes have a new sparkle. As I write now, the whole experience returns, suffusing my body with a sense of well being."

❖ Treat yourself to a healing session, using the guidelines listed above. When your healing session is complete, prepare to write about your experience.
  • In your journal, capture all the images, sensations, and feelings you can recall from your healing session. Write in the present tense. Use all your senses. Make your recall as vivid and real as you can to imprint it on your consciousness

I am convinced there as many healing blueprints as there are life challenges. We are only limited by our imaginations. Here are a few examples:
  • Rapid healing following trauma or surgery
  • Optimal eyesight
  • Conscious dying
  • Conscious birthing

- Clear, cognitive functioning
- Healthy relationships
- Creative expression
- Mastery
- Happiness
- Fulfillment of soul purpose

Give yourself permission to access and download as many genetic blueprints as you wish. Invite love to guide you as you reclaim your wholeness and healing.

Reflective Healing Questions

- What comforts, soothes, and replenishes your body?
- What is the most recent healing story you remember?
- What are your most cherished beliefs about healing and your healing potential?
- What are you willing to give up in order to heal?
- What is your healing vision for yourself? The planet?

Awakening Reflection Responses

I invite you to reflect on the Healing chapter and record your insights for this day.

- ❖ I Learned_____
- ❖ I Relearned_____
- ❖ I Discovered_____
- ❖ I Rediscovered_____
- ❖ I Regret_____
- ❖ I Appreciate_____
- ❖ Right Now I Feel_____
- ❖ And I Will_____

Journaling Prompts

Here are a few prompts to give you more to wrap your all-knowing heart around. Feel free to agree, disagree, make your own connections, or write your own quotations.

"Faith is the ability to sustain ambiguity." Lauren Artress

"Healing is not a cure but a better way to live with our wounds and restore a sense of meaning and purpose in our lives." Alan Briskin

"Epiphanies happen when life and death meet." Mark Matousek

"Forgiveness frees up energy for healing." Caroline Myss

"Miracles seem to rest, not so much upon faces or voices of healing power coming suddenly near to us from far off, but upon our perceptions being made finer so that for a moment our eyes can see and our ears can hear that which is about us always." Willa Cather

Conclusion

"We shall not cease from exploration
And the end of all our exploring,
Will be to arrive where we started
And know the place for the first time."
- T.S. Elliot

Love is the evolutionary driver in our School of Love. Mother Theresa once said, "We can do no great things, only small things with great love." I used to agree with her assessment of our human condition. However, I no longer believe that we are incapable of doing great things. I am convinced it is our authentic, multidimensional nature to express spaciousness and manifest miracles. I propose that we expand the curriculum in our School of Love to incorporate the 10 Cs proposed by Matthew Fox: cosmology, contemplation, chaos, courage, compassion, creativity, critical thinking, celebration, community, and character.

Awakening moves beyond the personal into the collective. In the process of moving beyond becoming and merging with being, we need each other. We need community where we are loved and honored for who we are as well as for our emergent authentic self. Within an evolutionary heart-centered community, we are conscious of what we are contributing to our personal energy field as well as what we are contributing to the emergent community energy field and beyond to the universal energy field

Rev. Dr. Martin Luther King, Jr. gave a talk at Western Michigan University on the theme of social justice and the emerging new age. Listen to his words: "All I'm saying is simply this, that all life is interrelated, that somehow we're caught in an inescapable network of mutuality tied in a single garment of destiny. Whatever affects one directly affects all indirectly. For some strange reason, I can never be what I ought to be until you are what you ought to be. You can never be what you ought to be until I am what I ought to be. This is the interrelated structure of reality."

Supported by community and grounded in self-love as well as love for others, we break through the force field of our own resistance and mediocrity to embrace our divine selves. Members of a heart-centered community serve as spiritual midwives for each other. Soul buddies grow into soul leaders. No longer will we be hypnotized by the voice of mediocrity, which says, "This is just the way it is and this is just the way I am."

We are expanding towards collaborative empowerment. The new paradigm invites us to become co-creators of a desired future. Each of us has the opportunity to move into the future with an embodied voice and an expansive vision that extends way beyond our personal transformation and embraces planetary transformation. According to Barbara Marx Hubbard, author of *Conscious Evolution: Awakening the Power of Social Potential,* "Conscious evolution happens when we make an individual and collective intention to grow in consciousness and use our increasing awareness to guide our actions and achieve a positive future. That reminds me of Gangaji's profound words, "You and the universe are lover and beloved."

According to George Leonard, "Evolution is the process through which the infinite possibilities of the human spirit are revealed. Extraordinary life often emerges as a gift rather than as the product of striving, because it was already there."

The three central questions asked by scholars at Chartres three hundred years ago still challenge us today:

- How can we, through connection with the spirit, heal the soul?
- How can we, working on the earth, heal our planet?
- How can we, through communion in the spirit, heal the body social?"

I know my soul's purpose calls upon me to integrate action and devotion in this lifetime. One without the support of the other lacks fulfillment, and my commitment to be an agent of evolutionary service feels limited rather than spacious. Please take a look at my homework assignment from an online course called Evolutionary Spirituality created by Craig Hamilton:

As a person who is committed to being a bridge between the future and Earth's present, here is what I know from experience to be possible. I know that love is all. I know that love opens the portals of possibility and heals. I know that intuition is the language of the heart and has the innate ability to provide the answers to our most urgent questions. I know, from my experience in the future, that our divinity is our birthright and everyone shares equally in this blessing. I know that personal and planetary evolution is grounded in service to the greater good and the well-being of all. I know that gratitude is the language of the soul, and each of us has many gifts of glory to add to the expansion of human consciousness. I know that love is the universal language, and the future of the evolution of the planets depends on each of us embracing each other and ourselves as lovers.

Looking from the future to your present, I see your future is made up of acts of love—blessings that multiply and magnify and inform your DNA that you are capable of creating anything that you can imagine. Peace and progress coexist in the future. Joy resounds with each act of kindness you extend to others. Service creates a greater inner experience of spaciousness that is reflected in the life you inhabit. Decision-making in all spheres of life is made from a consensus/inquiry perspective, and consulting the future ancestors is part of every major decision.

From the future, I know that music and light mirror one another and musicians play with light. Healing by downloading akashic blueprints will be as natural as brushing your teeth in the future. I also know that many future activists live among us in the present. They act as double agents: part of their service is to uplift our consciousness and part of their mission is to report back to the future so strategies can be designed to create more of the future in the present.

As I labored over how to summarize this book, I took a break to read my weekly astrological forecast, Planet Waves, by Eric Frances and laughed about the synchronicity with which the evolutionary impulse sometimes erupts. Eric wrote: "Have you ever had one of those revelations where you realize the one thing you need to do is relax, cease from exerting so much effort and energy and allow pure mind to get your results? That is, allow your consciousness to be the potent evolutionary agent that it is, and then experience the universe responding in its quantum way."

Surrendering to the energy of pure mind, I wrote: The present and the future invite each of us to become all that we already are! Our future ancestors as well as the evolution of our planet deserve to inherit a consciousness that is grounded, informed, and graced by our all-knowing hearts. As we surrender to the power of love and expand our willingness to love ourselves, each other, and the earth, we amplify our essential multidimensional natures and contribute to the healing and transformation of ourselves, each other, our communities, and our nations, as well as the healing of our planet. I invite you to let the future have her way with you.

Please take a gentle breath and return to your high heart as you read the following poem:

> You must give birth to your images.
> They are the future waiting to be born,
> Fear not the strangeness.
> The future must enter into you long before it happens.
> Just wait for the birth…
> For the hour of clarity."
> - Rainer Maria Rilke

I invite all of us to remember that our hearts are nourished by celebration and play, pleasure and beauty, creativity and laughter. Without your unique gifts and talents, the future will be less than it could be. The future is here now. Commit to growing your consciousness by loving all you are and all that surrounds you each day. Reach out to others and grow community. Imagine the future you wish for your grandchildren and their children to inherit and commit yourself to being an active agent for evolutionary consciousness. Thank you for your presence on earth at this crucial time of personal and evolutionary transformation. I look forward to joining my all-knowing heart with yours in service to humanity.

Appendix

Glossary

Acceleration: A movement toward the center.

Actualization: The courage to be the God within us.

Akashic records: A universal filing system that records each thought, word and action since the beginning of time.

Attention: Awareness that is focused and sharpened.

Blueprint: An energetic template.

Bleed-through lifetime: Overflow from an unintegrated past lifetime that influences one's ability to be fully conscious in this lifetime.

Cellular memory: A theory that 75 trillion cells in the body have various levels of shared information.

Coherence: To stick together, be united, interconnected

Consciousness: From the root "conscire," meaning "that which we know."

Co-arising: An energetic principle that explains the emergence of the polarity for whatever attribute one is affirming. Example: affirm love and expect whatever is the opposite of love to rise up.

Dimension: Invisible, organizing substructures within which we exist.

Discernment: An interior understanding of what is good or evil and how to act.

Energy frequency: The rate of vibration of a thought, feeling, or belief.

Enlightenment: An experience of the discovery of innate perfection of the present moment.

Epiphany: Flashes of sacred insight.

Essence: Sacred individuality.

Evolution: The journey of the soul as it grows through time and space.

Frequency: The vibrational rate of an energy field.

Grace: The spontaneous process by which unitive knowing, self-transcending love, and other extraordinary capacities emerge within us.

Harmony: A fluid state where Spirit manifests as matter.

Imbue: To inspire, permeate, and infuse.

Impeccability: The proper use of will.

Implicit memory: Traces of past experiences that exist beneath conscious awareness.

Imprint: To fix firmly in the mind or in one's cellular memory.

Inflation: The distance between one's self-knowledge and one's personal development.

Integrity: A commitment to be true to self, personal vision, and your unique form of service.

Intention: Focused attention derived from purposeful activation of the will.

Intuition: The silent voice of Spirit that connects the human self with the essence self.

Karma: The principle of cause and effect, or unfinished business carried over from one lifetime to the next.

Learned limitations: An internalized half-truth that limits alignment with essence.

Liminality: The transitional phase or period of a rite of passage during which the participant lacks social status or rank, remains anonymous, and follows prescribed forms of conduct.

Magic: The art of changing consciousness at will.

Merit: Positive results from actions.

Non-local: Existing not just in one place at one time but everywhere all the time.

Multi-dimensionality: The same phenomenon can be perceived from many perspectives.

Numinous: An experience of the sacred.

Organizing principles: Soul values that form the foundation of one's being.

Paradigm: A key pattern through which minor patterns are interpreted and coordinated.

Paradox: Truth standing on its head.

Psychic empathy: The capacity to merge with someone else and see the world through his or her eyes.

Quantum: The concept in physics of a realm of potentials where consciousness creates what will manifest in perceived reality.

Reciprocity: The state or condition that grants equal advantage and mutual exchange to all things and relationships.

Resonate: To amplify or to echo back when one energetic system vibrates in tune with another.

Self-actualization: The condition that emerges when capacity, action, and aspiration are in balance.

Serendipity: The faculty of making happy and unexpected discoveries by accident.

Soul agreements: Sacred contracts.

Soul: The divine spark within an individual that contains the cosmic blueprint for evolution.

Soul continuum: The evolutionary path marking a soul's growth and development.

Soul empowerment: Alignment of an individual with her/his soul's blueprint.

Spaciousness: Vast, uninterrupted space.

Spiritual bypass: A personality strategy that shortcuts the expression of pain and loss.

Spirit: The individual essence, the driving life force of an individual.

Symbolic Power: That which allows us to see things in impersonal terms, to view our own lives with a unity vision characteristic of the Aquarian Age, which calls for us to discover the inner power of consciousness.

Symbolic sight: Eternal sight containing all the truth ever acquired within the human experience.

Synchronicity: The coincidental occurrence of events, chance encounters, and evidence that an individual is in alignment with her/his soul's purpose.

Synergy: The natural principle of people joining together for a united purpose that creates a whole that is greater than the sum of its individual viewpoints or parts.

Template: A pattern.

Visualization: The use of imagination to gain intuitive insight.

Will: The inner drive to become conscious of one's self as a multidimensional creator.

Wisdom: Knowing that which embraces the truest feeling of the heart and the most profound seeing of the mind.

Meditations

Here are several meditations to add to your practice:

Feeling Meditation
I feel my body. My body feels me.
I feel my breath. My breath feels me.
I feel my feelings. My feelings feel me.
I feel my heart. My heart feels me.
I feel my guides. My guides feel me.
I feel the cosmos. The cosmos feels me.

Vacuum Cleaner Meditation
Before going to sleep, take a moment to stop and review all the thoughts that are hanging around in your mind. Now imagine you have a psychic vacuum cleaner and use it to remove any leftover thoughts. Good night!

Observant Bystander
Each time you are aware of a thought, start counting from one. Remember that "I don't have a thought" is a thought! A visualization counts as a thought.

Loving-kindness
Choose someone who has shown you extraordinary kindness and love.
Breathe in the essence of that loving kindness. Smile. Notice how strongly you are able to generate loving kindness. Extend loving-kindness

to people you care about. Then extend loving-kindness to neutral people. Then send out loving-kindness to people you have difficulty relating to.

I Don't Know Meditation

Let go of all the labels and names for everything. Walk around slowly, beholding everything as if for the first time.

Thich Nhat Hahn Meditation

Inhale: I have arrived. Exhale I am home.
Inhale, Listen. Exhale, Thank you.

Relax and Attend

Relax your body, relax your mind, and let go of any tension on all levels of your being. At the same time, make the effort to be as awake and attentive as possible. It is not necessary or helpful to pay attention to anything in particular. Simply pay attention to attention itself. Pay attention to what it is to be awake, conscious, and attentive. All the while, keep allowing yourself to relax more deeply.

Keep Your Heart Open to Love

Words and Music by
ROSALIE DEER HEART

Bibliography

Achterberg, Jeanne. *Imagery: Healing, Shamanism, and Modern Medicine.* Boston: Shambhala, 1985.

Achterberg, Jeanne, Dossey, Barbara, and Kolkmeier, Leslie. *Rituals of Healing: Using Imagery for Health and Wellness.* New York: Bantam Books, 1994.

Ardagh, Arjun. *Awakening into Oneness.* Sounds True, 2007.

Arrien, Angeles. *The Four Fold Way: Walking the Paths of Warrior, Teacher, Healer, and Visionary.* HarperOne, 1993.

Artress, Lauren. *Walking a Sacred Path: Rediscovering the Labyrinth as a Spiritual Tool.* New York: Riverhead Books, 1995.

Assaraf, John. *Having It All: Achieving Your Life's Goals and Dreams.* Atria, 2007.

Beckwith, Michael. *Spiritual Liberation: Fulfilling Your Soul's Potential.* New York: Atria Books, 2008.

Bentov, Itzhak. *Stalking the Wild Pendulum: On the Mechanics of Consciousness.* E. P. Dutton, New York, 1977.

Bolen, Jean, Shinoda. *The Tao of Psychology: Synchronicity and the Self.* New York: Harper & Row, 1979.

Braden, Gregg: *The Divine Matrix*. USA: Hay House, 2007.

Braden, Gregg. *The Spontaneous Healing of Belief: Shattering the Paradigm of False Limits*. USA: Hay House: 2008.

Briskin, Alan. *The Power of Collective Wisdom and the Trap of Collective Folly*. San Francisco: Berrett-Koehler Publishers, Inc. 2009.

Caddy, Eileen. *Open Doors Within*. Findhorn Press, 1976.

Cameron, Julia. *The Artist's Way*. Tarcher, 1992.

Carroll, Lee. *Transitioning Now: Redefining Duality 2012 and Beyond*. California: Red Wheel/Weiser, 2010.

Castenada, Carlos. *The Teachings of Don Juan*. Simon and Schuster, 1968.

Chittister, Joan. *Seeing with Our Souls: Monastic Wisdom for Every Day*. Maryland: Sheed and Wood, 2002.

Chopra, Depak, *Quantum Healing: Explaining the Frontiers of Mind/Body Medicine*. New York: Bantam Books, 1990.

Cohen, Alan. *The Dragon Doesn't Live Here Anymore*. Ballantine Books, 1993.

Craine, Renate. *Hildegard: Prophet of the Cosmic Christ*. New York: The Crossroad Publishing Company, 1997.

Daly, Ann, Lou. *Humans Being*. Authorhouse, 2009.

Dass, Ram. *Be Love Now: The Path of the Heart*. New York: Harper One, 2010.

Dossey, Larry. *Meaning and Medicine: Lessons from a Doctor's Tales of Breakthrough and Healing*. New York: Bantam Books, 1991.

Dossey, Larry. *Healing Words: The Power of Prayer and the Practice of Medicine.* San Francisco: Harper, 1993.

Dyer, Wayne. *The Power of Intention: Learning to Co-Create Your World, Your Way.* Carlsbad, California: Hay House, 2004.

Elgin, Duane. *The Living Universe: Who Are We? Where Are We Going?* USA: Berrett-Koehler Pub. 2009.

Erikson, Erik. *Gandhi's Truth.* W.W. Norton, 1993.

Ferrucci, Piero. *What We May Be.* Los Angeles: J.P. Tarcher, Inc., 1982

Ford, Debbie. The *Dark Side of the Light Chasers: Reclaiming Your Power, Creativity, Brilliance, and Dreams.* New York: Riverhead Books, 1998.

Fox, Matthew. *A Spirituality Named Compassion.* San Francisco: Harper & Row, 1990.

Frankl, Viktor, E. *The Doctor and the Soul: From Psychotherapy to Logotherapy.* New York: Alfred A. Knopf, 1968.

Gawain, Shakti. *Creative Visualization.* New World Library, 2002.

Gerber, Richard. *Vibrational Medicine: New Choices for Healing Ourselves.* Santa Fe: Bear and Company, 1988.

Griscom, Chris. *Ecstacy Is a Frequency.* Fireside Books, 1988.

Hafiz. *The Gift.* Penguin Compass, 1999.

Hahn, Thich Nhat. *The Present Moment: A Retreat on the Practice of Mindfulness (audio).* USA: Sounds True, 2003.

Hawkins, David. *Power vs. Force.* Sedona, Arizona: Veritas Publishing, 2000.

Heart, Rosalie Deer. *Healing Grief— Mother's Story.* San Cristobal, New Mexico, 1996.

Heart, Rosalie Deer and Strickland, Alison. *Harvesting Your Journals.* San Cristobal: New Mexico, 1999.

Heart, Rosalie Deer and Bradford, Michael. *Soul Empowerment.* San Cristobal, New Mexico, 1997

Helminski, Kabir. *The Knowing Heart: A Sufi Path of Transformation.* Boston: Shambhala, 1999.

Hornecker, John. *Quantum Transformation.* Lake Lure, North Carolina, 2011.

Houston, Jean. *Jump Time: Shaping Your Future in a World of Radical Change.* New York: Jeremy Tarcher/Putnam, 2000.

Hubbard, Barbara Marx. *Emergence: The Shift From Ego To Essence*: Charlotesville, Virginia: Hampton Roads, 2001.

Hubbard, Barbara Marx. *Conscious Evolution: Awakening the Power of Social Potential.* Novato, California: New World Library, 1998.

Jones, Alan. *Soul Making: The Desert Way of Spirituality.* San Francisco: Harper & Row, 1985.

Jones, James. *Transformational Practices Group Guide.* Virginia: Personal Awareness Institute, 2003.

Joy, Brugh. *Joy's Way: An Introduction to the Potentials for Healing with Body Energetics.* New York: Jeremy P. Tarcher/Putnam, 1979.

Judith, Anodea. *Waking the Global Heart: Humanities Rite of Passage the Love of Power to the Power of Love.* California: Elite Books, 2006.

Jung, Carl. *The Undiscovered Self.* Signet, 2006.

Katie, Byron. *Loving What Is: Four Questions that Can Change Your Life.* Three Rivers Press, 2003.

Keltner, Dacher. *Born to Be Good: The Science of a Meaningful Life*. New York: W.W. Norton and Company, 2009.

Kidd, Sue Monk. *When the Heart Waits: Spiritual Direction for Life's Sacred Questions*. San Francisco: HarperOne, 2006.

Kingdon, Kathlyn. *The Matter of Mind*. Arizona: Light Technology Publishing, 2007.

Kornfield, Jack. The *Wise Heart: A Guide to the Buddhist Universal Teachings of Psychology*. Bantam, 2009.

Laskow, Leonard. *Healing With Love: A Breakthrough Mind/Body Medical Program for Healing Yourself and Others*. USA: HarperCollins, 1992.

Leonard, George, and Murphy, Michael. *The Life We Are Given. A Long Term Program for Realizing the Potential of Body, Mind, and Soul*. New York: G.P. Putnam's Sons, 1995.

Lewis. Pepper. *Gaia Speaks—Sacred Earth Wisdom*. Light Technology Publishing. 2005.

Lilly, John. *The Center of the Cyclone*. New York: Julian Press, 1972.

Lipton, Bruce. *Matter and Miracles*. Santa Barbara, California: Love Books, 2005

Lipton, Bruce and Bhaerman, Steve. *Spontaneous Evolution: Our Positive Future (and a Way to Get There from Here)*. USA: Hay House, 2009.

Loori, John, Daido. *The Zen of Creativity: Cultivating Your Artistic Life*. New York: A Peekmouse Book: 2004

Macy, Joanna. *Coming Back to Life*. New Society Publishers, 1998.

Maharaj, Nisargadetta, Sri. *I Am That: Talks with Sri Nisargadatta Maharaj*. North Carolina: The Acorn Press, 1973.

Maisel, Eric. *The Van Gogh Blues: The Creative Person's Path through Depression*. New World Library, 2007.

Markova, Dawna. I *Will Not Die an Unlived Life: Reclaiming Purpose and Passion*. California: Conari Press, 2000.

Maslow, Abraham. *The Further Reaches of Human Nature*. Penguin, 1971.

Matousek, Mark. *When You Are Falling, Dive: Lessons in the Art of Living*. Bloomsbury USA. 2008.

McCartney, Francesca. *Body of Health: The Science of Intuitive Medicine*. California: New World Library, 2005.

Merton, Thomas. *Thoughts in Solitude*. New York: The Noonday Press, 1956.

Monroe, Robert. *Ultimate Journey*. New York: Doubleday, 1994

Moore, Thomas. *Care of the Soul*. Harper Pernnial, 1994.

Mountain Dreamer, Oriah, *What We Ache for: Creativity and the Unfolding of the Soul*. HarperOne, 2005.

Muktananda, Swami. *From the Finite to the Infinite*. SYDA Foundation, 1989.

Myss, Caroline. *Sacred Contracts: Awakening Your Divine Potential*. New York: Harmony Books, 2001

Myss, Caroline and Shealy, Norman. *The Creation of Health: The Emotional, Psychological, and Spiritual Response That Promotes Health and Healing*. New York: Three Rivers Press, 1988

Nearing, Helen and Scott. *Living the Good Life*. Schocken Books, 1990.

Norris, Kathleen. *Amazing Grace*. New York: Riverhead Books, 1998.

O'Donahue, John. *Beauty: Rediscovering the True Sources of Compassion, Serenity, and Hope.* USA: 2004.

Osborn, Arthur. *The Expansion of Awareness: One Man's Search for Meaning in Living.* India: The Theosophical Publishing House, 1961.

Palmer Parker Jan. A *Hidden Wholeness: The Journey Toward an Undivided Life.* California: Jossey-Bass, 2004.

Pearsall, Paul. *The Heart's Code: Tapping the Wisdom and Power of our Heart Energy.* New York: Broadway Books, 1998.

Peck, Scott. *The Road Less Traveled.* New York: Simon and Schuster, 1997.

Pert, Candace. *Molecules of Emotion: The Science Behind Mind-Body Medicine.* Simon and Schuster, 1999.

Phillips, Jan. *The Art of Original Thinking.* California: 9th Element Press, 2006.

Plotkin, Bill. Soul Craft: *Crossing Into the Mysteries of Nature and Psyche.* New World Library, 2008.

Riddell, Mark. *Sacred Journey: Spiritual Wisdom for Times of Transition.* Cleveland: The Pilgrim Press, 2001.

Roberts, Jane. *Seth Speaks: The Eternal Validity of Your Soul.* California: Amber Allen Publishers, 1972

Ruiz, Miguel. *The Four Agreements.* San Raphael, California. Amber Allen Publishers, 1997.

Rumi, Jalal al-Din. *The Essential Rumi.* HarperOne, 1997.

Sardello, Robert. *Love and the Soul: Creating a Future for the Earth.* New York: HarperCollins, 1995.

Selhub, Eva. *The Love Response.* Ballantine Books, 2009

Seligman, Martin. *Authentic Happiness: Using the New Positive Psychology to Realize Your Potential for Lasting Fulfillment.* Free Press, 2002.

Shealy, Norman and Church, Dawson. *Soul Medicine: Awakening Your Inner Blueprint for Abundant Health and Energy.* Santa Rosa, California: Psychology Press, 2006.

Siegel, Bernie. *Peace, Love, and Healing Mind/Body Communication: The Path to Self Healing.* New York: Harper & Row, 1989.

Spangler, David. *Everyday Miracles: The Inner Art of Manifestation.* New York: Bantam Books, 1996.

Stainetti, Frank. *Practical Awakening into Soul-Merging.* Spiritual Path Publishers, 2010.

Starhawk and Valentine, Hilary. *The Twelve Swans.* San Francisco: Harper, 2002

Vaughan, Frances. *Awakening Intuition.* USA: Anchor Books, 1979.

Welwood, John. *Perfect Love, Imperfect Relationships: Hiding the Wounds of the Heart.* Boston: Trumpeter, 2006.

Wheatley, Margaret. *Leadership and the New Science.* San Francisco: Barrett-Koehler Publishers, 1999.

Wheatley, Margaret and Kellner, Myron. *A Simpler Way.* San Francicso: Barrett Koehler Publishers, 1996.

Wilber, Ken. *A Brief History of Everything. Boston:* Shambhala*, 2001.*

Williamson, Marianne. *A Return of Love.* New York: Harper Collins, 1975.

Xarrian, Sasha. *Outrageous Mastery.*

Zukov, Gary. The *Seat of the Soul.* Free Press, 1990.

Author Biography

Rosalie Deer Heart celebrates life in all of its dimensions. She believes that the less we risk, the more we lose when we win. Her careers bridge many facets: teacher, psychotherapist, author, minister, sculptor, and licensed medium. She savors love, peace, nature, creativity, and stars.

Rosie lives in Maine with her daughter, two grandchildren, and three cats.

For more information about soul readings, retreats, workshops, and the We Are Peace Project, visit Rosalie's website at www.heart-soul-healing.com

Book Discussion Guide

Chapter One

Where do you mark the beginning of a spiritual journey in your own life? What is your experience of self-love?

Do you know people who practice leading their lives with love? How possible is it for you to step into each day affirming, "Love guides my life?" Is this a practical way to live?

The author uses School of Love as a metaphor. How closely does her metaphor match your understanding? What other metaphors occur to you? In what ways would your life be different if you imagined you were enrolled in a School of Love and learning about love was the only curriculum?

Do you agree that the love response can be an effective remedy for the stress response? How can you use the love response in your daily life?

Chapter Two

Why do you think the author bundled up many emotions and wrote a separate chapter? Isn't love an emotion?

How big a role does projection play in your life? What connections do you make with Djwahl Khul's statement, "Projections happen all the time and get in the way of authentic connections?" When have you experienced yourself projecting your version of reality upon another? How did that work out?

Brain research reminds us that when we transform our emotions, we change our brain. In what ways can you use this information to remind yourself to be emotionally present?

Do you agree that pain, whether mental, emotional, or spiritual is a resistance to your soul purpose? If you do, what difference will knowing this make in your daily life?

Chapter Three

According to the emerging theory of consciousness everything depends on how we see something. Can you connect a time in your life where two people experienced the same event and experienced different feelings and different meanings?

The author cites research that our beliefs affect our bodies. What evidence can you offer from your own life about the relationship of belief and its role in illness or well-being?

Do you agree with this statement by John Lilly, "It is my belief that the experience of higher states of consciousness is necessary for the survival of the human species?" What examples can you cite from your own life when you evolved a higher state of consciousness?

The author claims that karma conditions consciousness, and she includes several personal stories of past lifetime memories. How did you respond to her beliefs?

Chapter Four

Consider the statement, "Beliefs and intention support one another just like intention and manifestation support each other." How might that have played itself out in your life?

The author claims that our unconscious, counter intentions will always override our conscious intention. What evidence do you have from your own life to refute or support her statement?

Choosing faith over fear is one way to manifest your intentions. Has this strategy worked for you?

Embodying our intention is an essential skill in practicing the inner art of manifestation. Why?

Chapter Five

When in your life have you experienced following your intuition? What did you give up and what did you gain?

The author claims that intuition connects us to the universal mind. Do you agree? Why?

The author connects intuition, spirituality, and creativity and refers to them as "The Three Sisters." What do you think of her claim that those aspects are intimately connected? Is that true for you?

In what ways have you opened to your intuition as a result of reading this book?

Chapter Six

Do you agree with the author that embodied spirituality is grounded in being open hearted? What does embodied spirituality mean to you?

Ego is described as trickster in this chapter. Do you agree that dissolving the ego is the work of the soul? What is the role of love in dissolving the ego?

The author makes a case for making a commitment to a spiritual practice in order to connect more deeply with your all-knowing heart. What is your experience with spiritual practices? What do you desire concerning spiritual practice as you move forward?

Do you agree that your soul purpose evolves as your consciousness evolves? Looking back on your life, can you identify how a shift or expansion of consciousness affected your soul purpose?

Chapter Seven

How has creativity contributed to new understandings about who you are? In what ways has your practice of creativity empowered you?

What is your experience with expressing gratitude? Were you surprised by the research findings of Dr. Martin Seligman that stated that gratitude decreased depression?

How has your unique form of creativity called you? How does your creative expression connect you with your spiritual life?

The author makes a distinction between inspiration and motivation in relationship to creativity. Does her distinction fit your experience?

Chapter Eight

What are your personal experiences of healing? Do you agree that multidimensional healing restores wholeness and harmony? Why?

Many people agree that illness as a wake up call from our soul. How does that connect with your experience?

Alan Briskin says that all healing is relational, and the quality of our relationships either promotes well-being or contributes to illness and disease. Do you agree?

Holographic healing encompasses our multidimensional nature and bridges both past and future lifetimes. What was your response to the idea of downloading blueprints from your akashic records to promote healing?

Also by Rosalie Deer Heart

Affective Education Guidebook: Classroom Activities in the Realm of Feelings with Bob Eberle

Affective Direction: Planning and Teaching for Thinking and Feeling with Bob Eberle

Healing Grief: A Mother's Story

Harvesting Your Journals: Writing Tools to Enhance Your Growth and Creativity with Alison Strickland

Soul Empowerment: A Guidebook for Healing Yourself and Others with Michael Bradford

Celebrating the Soul of CPSI with Dorie Shallcross

CPSIA information can be obtained at www.ICGtesting.com
Printed in the USA
268212BV00002B/2/P